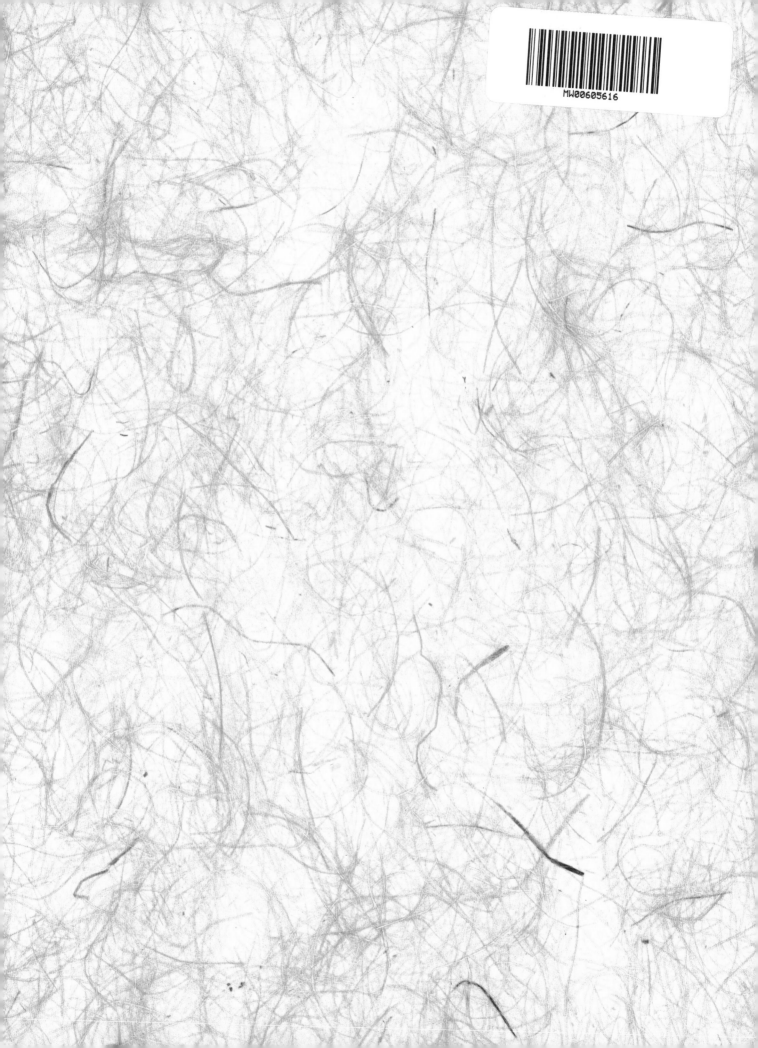

MW00605616

The Artistic Glassware
of Dalzell, Gilmore, and Leighton

Jo & Bob Sanford
and Barbara & Jim Payne

Schiffer Publishing Ltd

4880 Lower Valley Road, Atglen, PA 19310 USA

Dedication

This book is dedicated to Charlotte McGee.

Other Schiffer Books by Jo & Bob Sanford
Victorian Glass Novelties

Other Schiffer Books on Related Subjects
The Black Glass Encyclopedia, The West Virginia Museum of American Glass, Ltd.
Great Art Glass Lamps: Tiffany, Duffner & Kimberly, Pairpoint, and Handel, Martin M. May.
Victorian Decorative Glass, British Designs, 1850-1914, Mervyn Gulliver.

Copyright © 2006 by Jo & Bob Sanford and Barbara & Jim Payne
Library of Congress Control Number: 2006926229

All rights reserved. No part of this work may be reproduced or used in any form or by any means—graphic, electronic, or mechanical, including photocopying or information storage and retrieval systems—without written permission from the publisher.
The scanning, uploading and distribution of this book or any part thereof via the Internet or via any other means without the permission of the publisher is illegal and punishable by law. Please purchase only authorized editions and do not participate in or encourage the electronic piracy of copyrighted materials.
"Schiffer," "Schiffer Publishing Ltd. & Design," and the "Design of pen and ink well" are registered trademarks of Schiffer Publishing Ltd.

Designed by Mark David Bowyer
Type set in Bodoni Bd BT / Cooper Lt BT

ISBN: 0-7643-2523-X
Printed in China
1 2 3 4

Published by Schiffer Publishing Ltd.
4880 Lower Valley Road
Atglen, PA 19310
Phone: (610) 593-1777; Fax: (610) 593-2002
E-mail: Info@schifferbooks.com

For the largest selection of fine reference books on this and related subjects, please visit our web site at
www.schifferbooks.com
We are always looking for people to write books on new and related subjects. If you have an idea for a book please contact us at the above address.

This book may be purchased from the publisher.
Include $3.95 for shipping.
Please try your bookstore first.
You may write for a free catalog.

In Europe, Schiffer books are distributed by
Bushwood Books
6 Marksbury Ave.
Kew Gardens
Surrey TW9 4JF England
Phone: 44 (0) 20 8392-8585; Fax: 44 (0) 20 8392-9876
E-mail: info@bushwoodbooks.co.uk
Website: www.bushwoodbooks.co.uk
Free postage in the U.K., Europe; air mail at cost.

Contents

Acknowledgments

We appreciate the contributions of:

Corning Museum of Glass, Gail Bardham
Ron Baker
Neila and Tom Bredehoft
Carole and Bob Bruce
Patricia and Bob Costa
Thornton Grubb
Ted Hindall
Larry Loxterman
Dennis P McGee

Jim & Birdie McGee
Ron McMillen
Douglas Millhoff
Minnesota Historical Society Library, Steve Nielsen,
    Reference Associate
Robert Tong
Karen and Jerry Volkmer
The staff of the Volusia County Public Library, Deland,
    Florida
Loren Weyant
Richard White

Preface

This book provides a history of the Dalzell, Gilmore and Leighton Glass Company. It started in 1883 when the company was first organized by Andrew C. James, W. A. B. Dalzell, and E. D. Gilmore. The name of the firm was Dalzell and Gilmore.

While erecting a new factory at Wellsburg, West Virginia, they leased the old Brilliant Glass Works at Brilliant, Ohio. Many problems were encountered during the construction of the new factory, including a flood, and operation began in 1885.

In the year of 1888, a gas boom had taken place in northern Ohio and many incentives were given to manufacturers to persuade them to relocate to the natural gas area. Thus, the company made the move from Wellsburgh, West Virginia, to Findlay, Ohio. The company naturally moved their pattern molds with them and so there are patterns, novelties, and lamps that were manufactured at all three locations. This book will not attempt to determine which of the three factories produced a specific piece of glass and here is why. To pick a piece of glass from one of these items and say definitely that it was manufactured at this site or that site would be foolhardy. What this means is that if you like a piece of glass, then the site of manufacture means nothing to anyone except a researcher.

James Dalzell

Andrew Dalzell

W. A. B. Dalzell

In this book, we have attempted to find the original factory name for each pattern and, when successful, we will use it. We will, however, use the collector name also to avoid confusion. Most of the pattern names evolved from the writings of Don Smith, the original researcher of glassware made in Findlay, Ohio. Without the research of Don Smith to lead the way, we probably wouldn't be writing this book. Don shared information over the years and we were happy to call him a friend. He will always be missed.

About the Values

The values placed on the items in this book were gathered from dealers who exhibit at major antiques shows in the United States and from collectors who have specialized collections. These values will vary in different sections of the country and values will fluctuate, as dealers usually must pay higher prices as they replenish their stock and they in turn must make a small profit. This is strictly an estimated value guide and must not be used as a buying guide. Please be advised that the values for Floradine and Onyx in color are changing almost daily.

The best guide to buying when starting to collect is to know and trust the dealer that you are buying from.

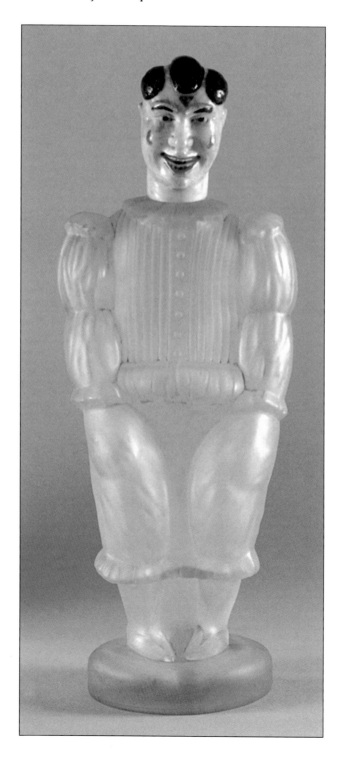

Dalzell, Gilmore, and Leighton Company

The History

An article appeared in the *Crockery and Glass Journal* dated April 19, 1888, with the news that: *The natural gas towns in the interior of Ohio and Indiana are making great efforts to boom things this spring again and have quite a number of manufacturers on the "qui vive". Dalzell Bros. & Gilmore, of Wellsburgh, have contracted to put up a factory at Findlay, and other negotiations are pending. The real estate owners and agents form such syndicates that they give large cash bonuses in addition to the land and gas, and as soon as the contracts are signed for a new factory they begin to advertise that 500 additional inhabitants will be there inside of sixty days, and up goes the price of lots on the farms they have laid out.*

A new plant was erected at Findlay, Ohio, in 1888 with James Dalzell, W. A. B. Dalzell, the estate of Andrew Dalzell (Andrew had died two weeks before the move), E. D. Gilmore, William Leighton, Jr., and his son George Leighton. With the addition of William Russell as plant manager, they had some of the most knowledgeable glass men and chemists (metal makers) in the industry making their wares.

Factory letterhead

Brick buildings were erected that included a mixing room, tempering ovens, two eleven-pot tableware furnaces, and glory holes. The furnace room had a brick floor. By November, the firm had added and was firing their third furnace. The buildings were engineered or designed all for fast and easy handling of the materials upon arrival and through to the shipping of the end product. At this time, the products were tableware and lamps. Gas was available free from the company's own well, which had been furnished them as an incentive. The city retained ownership of the well. This was a great expense saver as much gas was used in the production of glass.

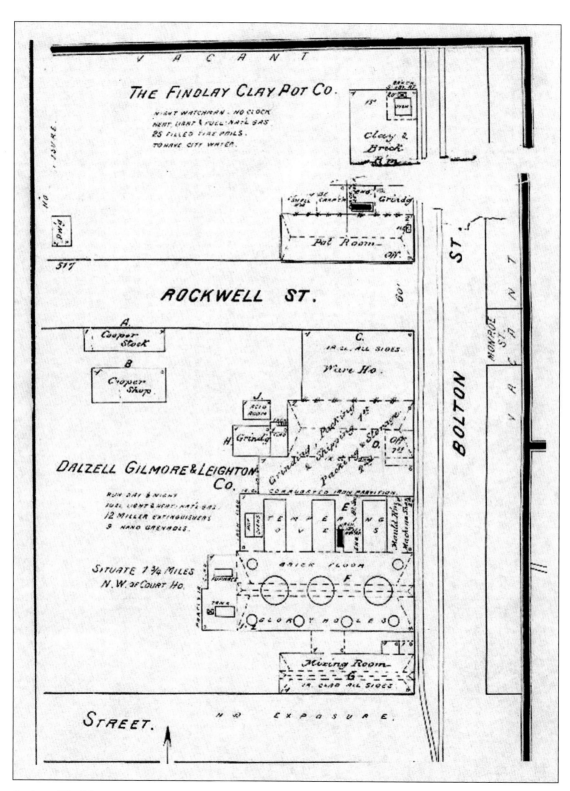

Sanborn Fire Map

The City and the Glass Manufacturers

A report of problems that the glass manufacturers had was documented in the trade journals. One such instance appeared in *The Crockery & Glass Journal* of December 12, 1890:

The suit of Dalzell, Gilmore & Leighton Company vs. Colonel John W. Harper et al, which had been on trial for a week before Judge Moore and a jury, resulted in a verdict for the plaintiffs. The plaintiffs erected a $100,000 glass plant in Findlay on consideration of a guarantee by five land syndicates of a cash bonus of $10,000, to be paid within thirty days after the plant was in operation, $2,500 additional when 250 men were employed, a second $2,500 when 300 men were employed, and deeds to the grounds on which the plant is located. The deeds were executed and all but $2,300 was paid of the $10,000 first to become due on the bonus. The suit was for recovery of the $2,300 and the two sums of $2,500 each, which, it was claimed, had also become payable. The defendants were John W. Harper, E.T. Dunn, Joseph Ramsey, Jr., T.H. McConica and W.B. Ely, representing the five syndicates. There was a big fight to take the case from the jury, largely on the ground that the plaintiffs were not identical with the parties with whom the contract was made, but had acquired the contract by assignment. The motion was overruled, and the case went to the jury on the question of consent to the change of parties to the contract, and also as to whether the required number of men had been employed at the factory. The jury found the amount still due on the bonus to be $4,971.63. Robert Ramsey for plaintiff.

It seems that the glass manufacturers never had smooth sailing because problems with gas supplies started in 1891. From an article that appeared in *China, Glass & Lamps* on January 7, 1891, we learn that: *At a meeting of the gas trustees at Findlay, O., it was resolved to notify all factories that after January 1 only eight ounces of pressure would be allowed at the factories, and all pipes and connections to furnaces to be put in according to plans to be furnished by the superintendent. It was agreed that hereafter private consumers could have gas at ten cents per thousand and furnish their own meters, which would be supplied at wholesale prices.*

In reference to this, it was also reported that: *The gas trustees wanted to cut off the Model Flint Glass Company, the Columbia Glass Company, the Bellaire Goblet Company, and Dalzell, Gilmore & Leighton Company all who have special contracts with the town. These companies and others applied for an injunction in the courts.*

The following is found in *China, Glass & Lamps* of January 14, 1891:

Eight injunctions were issued by Judge Johnson, at Bowling Green, on December 31, restraining the gas trustees of this town from shutting off the supply of natural gas from those factories which claimed to have contracts with the city and refused to pay the increased assessment of the gas board. The glass factories that secured injunctions were: The Columbia Glass Co., Dalzell, Gilmore & Leighton Co., Model Flint Glass Co., Lippencott Chimney Co., Bellaire Goblet Co., and the Findlay Window Glass Co. A motion for the dissolution of the injunction was to have been heard by Judge Johnson at Kenton on Wednesday last. The Findlay Republican *of January 1 has the following details of the questions at issue in the contest ' The question of legality of the contracts held by the factories is one which will give opportunity for much legal study and argument, and the contest over them will be full of interest. Each of these companies holds a contract either with the city gas trustees or with the old gas light company, which assigned its effects to the city when its plant was purchased. Several of the contracts were not made with the factories now holding them, but were made with land syndicates who assigned them to the present holders. All but three of the contracts are in the nature of resolutions by the board in past years. Another point is that no two of them are precisely alike in wording or detail and it may be a question whether a decision that one is good will have the effect of settling the character of all of them. Most of them are conditioned on the supply of gas holding out, and the trustees doubtless hold that the gas has not held out, at least in the same proportion as to supply and cost of furnishing it. At least one of the contracts stipulates that if the trustees are compelled to go outside of the city to drill wells that the factory in question must bear its proportion of the expense of the piping required. It will be seen from this that there are a number of questions which will have a bearing on the case and that a decision on each of the contracts may be necessary, unless, indeed, the court should hold that cities are not allowed to furnish gas or any other commodity at less than cost and on that ground hold all contracts based on such uncertain stipulations as the supply of natural gas to be illegal. There has been considerable difference of opinion as to what was the proper mode of getting a decision on the legality of the contracts. The gas trustees when making their new schedule three months ago decided to ignore the matter of contracts and consider them as annulled. Those holding them, however, were of course not satisfied to accept a decision of that kind and refused to pay more than the rate called for by their contracts. The trustees did not* take prompt action by suit to collect the rate they had assessed but allowed the matter to stand open. Their idea has been to force the holders of the contracts to take the initiative step to secure a decision from the courts, and with that view have threatened to shut off those not paying up. The factories, however, have taken the ground that it was proper for the gas trustees to make the test, and have suggested that instead of shutting all of them off and closing their business that the trustees bring suit against some one factory and endeavor to collect the increased assessment. The trustees have not agreed to this but at their meeting last week decided to notify those who refused to pay that all delinquent by January 1st would be cut off, this has had the effect desired by the trustees and the contract holders have taken steps to secure injunctions.

Production Starts

The Dalzell, Gilmore and Leighton Company commenced making glass on September 6, 1888, with one furnace. By the end of the month, the second and third furnaces were in operation. In November, they had started making holiday goods, which included some elegant designs in ruby and opalescent shades, and other goods in rich colors. It was announced at this time that Mr. Charles H. Lambie, of Pittsburgh, Pennsylvania, had associated with the firm as a partner.

The year 1889 was a year to be remembered, because this firm was assigned the patent by George Leighton to start producing Onyx and Floradine ware. Although they had many problems with this production and stopped in about ten months, there is no proof that this venture drove them to near bankruptcy. In fact, there is no proof that they were near bankruptcy at all. There were always rumors around the glass industry and this was probably another.

The constant worry for the glass industry in Findlay was the availability of gas. From the *Crockery and Glass Journal* of April 21, 1892, it is reported that: *The men who have money invested in the manufacture of glass in this city have been very nervous over the prospect of not having enough gas for their needs. It has been short all winter, but last Friday the City Gas Co. opened a bad six inch gate at one of the regulating stations, and it is said that within ten minutes the pressure at every factory was increased by over twenty pounds.*

The gas shortages continued and the result was nearly disastrous. As reported in *China, Glass & Lamps* on January 18, 1893 – *After seven years of plentiful supply, the Board of Trustees of the city of Findlay, Ohio, turned the key to the mains on January 11 and shut off the gas from all manufacturing establishments there. The ostensible reason for this action was the necessity for economizing the supply for the use of private consumers, but it appears that this point has not been gained, and the condition of the latter has not been improved in the least. Dalzell, Gilmore & Leighton Co. acted the part of the wise virgins and had their oil plant ready to avert disaster; the Model Flint Glass Co. were allowed enough gas to keep their pots warm until they had oil connections completed, but the Bellaire Goblet Works, the Columbia Glass Works and the plant of the United Glass Co. were not prepared for the sudden deprivation of fuel and suffered much loss in consequence. The manufacturers generally denounce the cutting off of the gas as an outrageous act and say that some of the factories will never resume work again. They also make the pertinent query: — if manufacturing establishments are discouraged and driven from the city, where will the private consumers be, for whose alleged benefit the gas was taken from the manufacturers? The majority of these consumers are dependent on the industries of the place for a living and if these industries cease, what becomes of the army of workers they have gathered about them and the various business enterprises these toilers support?* It should be noted that the writer of this article misstated that there was another U. S. Glass factory other than the Bellaire Goblet Works and the Columbia Glass Works. These two factories were never restarted.

James Dalzell

In February of 1893, the firm was saddened by the loss of one of their founders. We are placing the report as was written in *China, Glass & Lamps*: —*Mr. James Dalzell, one of the best-known flint manufacturers in the country, died on Tuesday, February 21, in Wellsburg, W. Va. Mr. Dalzell was born on the Southside, Pittsburgh, 39 years ago. He was educated in the Pittsburgh schools, and his early manhood was spent in this city. His career in the glass business commenced when he began as a bookkeeper for the firm of Adams & Co., where his business ability and manly straight-forward habits soon earned him an interest in the business. Leaving the firm of Adams & Co., he, in the company of his brothers, founded a glass house in Wellsburgh, the firm being Dalzell Bros. & Gilmore. After the natural gas discovery at Findlay, Ohio, the plant was removed to that place, where it is still operated by the Dalzell, Gilmore & Leighton Co. In 1887 Mr. Dalzell married Annie Duval, daughter of General I. H. Duval, of Wellsburgh at whose home he died. His wife and two small children survive him. While in Pittsburgh Mr. Dalzell was a member of the Bingham Street Methodist Episcopal Church. He was an amiable and charitable man in all his dealings and was a favorite with all on account of his urbanity, affability and strictly upright character.*

With the death of James Dalzell, the vacancy of his presidency was filled by his brother, W. A. B. Dalzell.

Alternate Fuels

In June of 1893 the rumors were rampant that Dalzell, Gilmore & Leighton Co. was contemplating removal from Findlay. But, as usual, it was strictly a rumor.

Always in search of being prepared for emergencies, the firm had always sought alternate fuels. In *China, Glass & Lamps*, an article dated October 2, 1895, revealed: *Dalzell, Gilmore & Leighton Co. have 'struck it rich' with their new gas producer system. It makes gas from Ohio coal for use under the boilers, in two furnaces, glory holes and lehrs, and works with perfect satisfaction.* The firm had earlier been using oil as their fuel when the natural gas was to be turned off, but it was proven to be too expensive. The company was no longer at the mercy of the gas and oil industry and no longer concerned about having to stop operations because of gas shortages.

In January of 1898, the firm had another rumor to dispel. This time a rumor was being passed that they weren't cooperating with jobbers. The firm made a public statement addressing the rumor and verified that their entire trade *lies with the jobbing houses, and they are one of the concerns that have always lived up to their agreement with the jobbers.*

Inventions

The years of 1898 and 1899 were a time of great things for this firm, thanks to the inventiveness of W. A. B. Dalzell and Philip Ebeling. A patent was registered to Mr. Dalzell on February 6, 1898, for a force fit lamp collar, Patent No. 642,307. This collar was similar to the Riverside clinch on collar and can be easily confused with it. The shape is nearly the same, including the flange; however, whereas the flange on the Riverside collar seems to rest on the font, there is a small space between the flange and the font on the Dalzell collar. The Dalzell collar will not have the clinch mark, as it was a force fit collar. This process was also adapted for a syrup lid. A second invention was a machine for applying the force on collars. This was an invention by Philip Ebeling; Patent No. 642,307 dated July 10, 1899. A third, and probably the most important, was Patent No. 653,412 by Philip Ebeling for making lamps. This was a machine that would make lamps in one piece. Two trade journal articles describe the importance of these inventions. Noted by *China, Glass & Lamps*, dated April 27, 1899, we find: *The Dalzell, Gilmore & Leighton Co., Findlay, O., has for years been known as manufacturers of generally pressed lines, tableware and lamps, but for some time past have added largely to their lines of specialties, and have introduced new processes and mechanical devices which enable them to make clearer, more uniform and superior finished goods at lowest cost of production, and these features have given their goods a large and steady demand. In their line of glass lamps, their blown on collars are among the special features of their line, while their machine blown molasses cans have not only surprised competing manufacturers but have astonished some of the oldest jobbers in the business by their uniformity, fine finish, and smooth, closed in bottoms. A full new line of lamps and syrup cans are being prepared for the fall trade, and the special machinery will be used in their manufacture.* On July 6, 1899 it was reported that: *Dalzell, Gilmore & Leighton, the Findlay, O, glass manufacturers are at present running two excellent specialties, which are being well made by patented machinery, owned exclusively by this firm. Syrup cans of all sizes, with pressed glass lip, pressed figure and pressed, smooth bottom, are now being made by machinery, by a process which practically revolutionizes the manufacture of this class of ware. In glass lamp manufacture, the firm has perfected machinery which they have been experimenting with for several years, and they are now making one piece, all glass lamps of superior quality, with clinched on, or rather, metal imbedded blown in collars, warranted oil and air tight, and non detachable. These goods have had a large sale wherever introduced, and have given exceptional satisfaction to the trade. Orders for the fall, should be placed early, as these goods are certain to have a very large sale, and will prove leaders in their line.*

The National Glass Company

In 1899 many of the independent flint glassware factories were having problems trying to compete with the mammoth United States Glass Company. There were rumors for many months about the formation of a new combine and late in the year it became a fact. The Dalzell, Gilmore & Leighton Company was sold to the National Glass Company for $200,000 on October 14, 1899, and became their No. 6 Glass Works.

With the sale of the firm to the National Glass Company, Ed Gilmore decided to leave the glass industry and became associated with the Pittsburg Trust Company. Mr. Gilmore had been associated with the industry since the founding of the Dalzell and Gilmore Glass Company at Wellsburg, West Virginia.

The National Glass Company wanted to purchase Dalzell, Gilmore & Leighton for their lamp machinery and forced fit collars. They wanted them for use at their two other lamp-producing companies, McKee Brothers Glass Works of Jeanette, Pennsylvania, and the Ohio Flint Glass Works at Lancaster, Ohio.

The trade journal *China Glass & Lamps* of March 22, 1900, included the information that: *The National Glass Company, report an active average demand for their various Products. All their plants are in full blast.*

The Dalzell, Gilmore & Leighton plant at Findlay, O. was so overcrowded with orders recently that they were compelled to turn some of them over to other factories. Everything is moving along harmoniously and the outlook is bright for a good demand right along. This is evidently when The National Glass Co. transferred molds of several novelties and pitchers to the I.T. & G. Glass Works at Greentown, Indiana.

Factory Closings

It soon became apparent that the National Glass Company had a desire to eliminate many of the glass works. A new factory was erected at Cambridge, Ohio, and was independent from the combine. The plan was to avail the Cambridge factory with the best of the combine glass works' and have a modern, competitive factory.

The end of the Factory 6 Glass Works at Findlay, Ohio, was now imminent and all that remained was the question of a date for closing. The answer we find in *China, Glass & Lamps* of November 16, 1901. It is written that: *There is no longer much question but what the National Glass Co. will abandon their Findlay, O., plant when their new Cambridge, O., factory is ready. All the present force at Findlay is to be transferred, and it is likely that the Findlay plant will be abandoned, though no definite announcement has been made. The mold makers at the Findlay plant are busy making molds for the following goods to be made at Cambridge: Two complete lines of tableware, two lamp lines and a new line of Hoffman House goblets. The press shops at the company's Lancaster, O., plant, are to be sent to Cambridge, which the National proposes to make the most complete plant in the country. China, Glass & Lamps* December 7, 1901, states in their final article about the closing that: *The Dalzell, Gilmore & Leighton plant, at Findlay, O., was abandoned Saturday by the National Glass Co., and it will be dismantled as quickly as possible, and most of the equipment will be moved to Cambridge, O., to be placed in the new plant there. A portion of the fittings of the Findlay factory will be transferred to the Riverside Glass Works at Wellsburg, W. Va.*

Special attention should be paid to the fact that molds made for the Cambridge factory are the only molds mentioned. We do know from National Glass Company catalogs that the lamp molds were transferred to the Ohio Flint Glass Works at Lancaster, Ohio, because of the National Glass Company catalog illustrations of known Dalzell, Gilmore & Leighton lamps being made at the Lancaster Works. Since the Cambridge factory was not completed at the closing of the Findlay Works it is evident that the Lancaster works remained open and producing glassware, including lamps. We know by the Dalzell, Gilmore & Leighton catalog of 1895 and the Cambridge catalog of 1903 that several molds were transferred to Cambridge. The 15D Molasses Can with the glass lip became the Cambridge #2525 Molasses Jug. The 5D 14 oz. and 16-1/2 oz. Molasses Cans became the Cambridge #2527 and 2528 Molasses Cans.

We know that several of the novelty molds had been sent to the National Glass Works # 9 at Greentown, Indiana, because of colors of items made and collected and shards in colors of glass that were made at that factory have been found for several novelties, including pitchers. There is some doubt about the Squirrel pitcher, however, because the pattern and shape are not identical.

With the documented information that is available, we cannot say for certain what happened to the other Findlay molds, cullet or the glassware in their warehouse. Any speculation would be only guesses and would have very little value. For example, we know that clear glass shards (cullet) cannot be used for positive attribution because cullet is used in the making of glass. Clear shards (cullet) could easily be purchased and shipped as a commodity for the manufacture of glass. Therefore the appearance of clear shards being found at a location other than the place of manufacture does not confirm that the glass was made at that location.

It is also known that factory products cannot be attributed by the illustrations in wholesaler's catalogs because some group illustrations include products of different factories. For example, an unidentified pitcher is illustrated, in a December 1901 Butler Brothers catalog (page 195), with the U. S. Glass Co. Oregon pattern. It is not the pitcher of this pattern. On page 198 of the same catalog, this unidentified pitcher is illustrated with National Glass Company pitchers. There are many other examples that could be given.

The Products

Wellsburgh Patterns

The first production items were the same as they were manufacturing at Wellsburgh. This included patterns 5D, which was plain for engraving in a Molasses Can, Cake Salver, and a 1/2 Gallon Pitcher; 6D in a Molasses Can and 1/2 Gallon Pitcher; 7D, 11D, 14D, 16D, which were Jelly Tumblers; 9D, a Grape and Current Goblet; 13D, a Swirl Goblet; 17D, the Six Panel Finecut pattern; 21D, the Starred Block pattern; and the 25D pattern of Ring and Swirl. There were many more plain goblets and tumblers, as were illustrated in an 1895 catalog by this firm. To view these various items, this catalog is available at the Corning Museum of Glass.

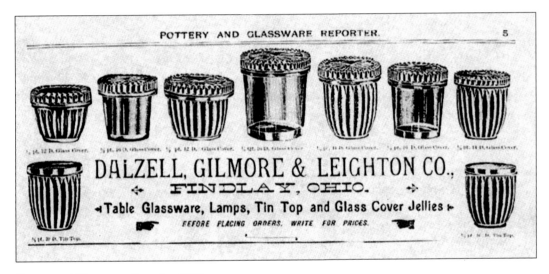

Pottery and Glassware Reporter, 1890

Pottery and Glassware Reporter, 1890

Pattern No. 5D is a plain pattern made in Syrup Pitchers, Tumblers, and Goblets. The Syrups were made with tin tops, one with their patented Drip Top.

Ogden, Merrill & Greer
catalog, 1895

5. Tin Top, $1.50.

Ogden, Merrill & Greer
catalog, 1895

5. Pat. Drip. Tin Top, $1.50, Nickel, $2.50

Pattern No. 6D is a beautiful pattern, as seen in the following illustrations. This pattern exists in Syrup Pitchers, Tumblers, and Goblets. As with the 5D pattern, the 6D pattern also was made in Syrup Pitchers with the tin top, and also with the tin top Drip Patent lids.

Ogden, Merrill & Greer catalog, 1895

6. Tin Top, $1.50.

6. Patent Drip.
Tin Top, $1.80; Nickel Top, $2.50.

Ogden, Merrill & Greer catalog, 1895

Pattern No. 10D is a Syrup Pitcher that was available with the standard tin top and also the Patent Drip top.

Pattern No. 15D is a Syrup Pitcher with a glass lip and the top hinged through the glass.

10. Tin Top .... $1.50.
10. Patent Drip. Nickel Top, $2.50.

Ogden, Merrill & Greer catalog, 1895

15. Glass Lip. Cheap, $2.75.

Ogden, Merrill & Greer catalog, 1895

Pattern No. 17D,
a.k.a. Six Panel Finecut

One of the patterns that the company continued after moving to Findlay was pattern #17D. Collectors call it Six Panel Finecut. This pattern was first introduced in 1885 and was so popular that illustrations can be found in Butler Brothers catalogs into the 1890s. It can be found with engraving on the plain parts, amber stain within these engravings, and amber stain bars in the pattern.

G. Sommers & Co. catalog, 1887

G. Sommers & Co. catalog, 1886

Pieces to be found in Six Panel Finecut include Covered Butter, Covered Sugar, Cream Pitcher, Spoon Holder, Squat Water Pitcher, Tankard Water Pitcher, Milk Pitcher, Celery Vase, Goblet, Wine, Tumbler, Water Tray, Salt Shaker, Sugar Shaker, Molasses Jug, Cake Salver, Berry Set, 7" and 8" Open Compotes, and 7" and 8" Covered Compotes.

Six Panel Finecut Pitcher, tankard, $70-125.

Six Panel Finecut Goblet, 6" high, 3" wide, $35-45.
Six Panel Finecut Wine, amber stain engraved flowers, 3 1/2" high, 1 5/8" wide, $35-45.
Six Panel Finecut Goblet, amber stain bars, $45-55.

Six Panel Finecut Salt & Pepper shakers, amber stain bars, $75-95 pr.

Six Panel Finecut Tumbler, engraved amber stain flowers, $50-65.

Six Panel Finecut Covered Butter, amber stain bars, $135-165.

Six Panel Finecut Compotes, amber stain bars, high standard, $125-150.

Six Panel Finecut Pitcher, bulbous, engraved, amber stain, $145-170.
Six Panel Finecut Goblet, engraved, amber stain bars, $45-55.
Six Panel Finecut Tumbler, amber stain bars, $50-65.

Six Panel Finecut #2 Lamp, amber stain, $250-325.

Pattern No. 21D,
a.k.a. Starred Block

Another of the patterns made at Wellsburgh and continued at the Findlay factory was the #21D or Starred Block pattern. This is the only Daisy and Button type pattern manufactured by this firm. Some collectors have referred to this pattern as Petticoat Band.

Wallace & Company catalog, 1887

JELLY STAND & COVER

7 & 8 IN. BOWL

211 CELERY ENG. E

FOOTED OVAL DISH

SUGAR

7 & 8 IN. BOWL

CREAM

BUTTER

Starred Block Tankard Pitcher, $110-145.

Starred Block Pedestalled Butter Dish, covered, $185.

Starred Block Compotes, covered, $85-95 ea.

Starred Block Hat, novelty made from a tumbler, $55-70.

Our "GENTEEL" 50-Cent Assortment.

Three Massive Products in Art Glassware.

This splendid assortment of 50-cent glassware is composed of three articles which, separately or together, would stand for the highest results in the glassworker's art. Large pieces, elegant designs.

THE ASSORTMENT COMPRISES 1-3 DOZEN EACH OF THE FOLLOWING:

Hand Engraved Half Gallon Pitchers—Massive 50-cent table gems.
8-Inch High-Footed Bowls—With 9-inch outside cover.
9-Inch Heavy Fancy Salvers—Surpassingly elegant regal beauties.

......Order here.   (*Total of* zen *to package, sold only by package.*)   Price, $3.55 Doz.

Butler Brothers catalog, 1892

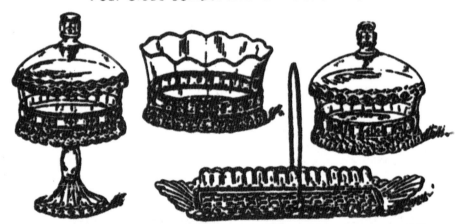

Our "ARLINGTON" 25-Cent Assortment.
Four Close Competitors for Public Favor.

It has seemed impossible to equal in the glassware market of America many of the assortments which in the past have become famous by our enormous purchases. This one, however, will be considered by some to *surpass* all our previous offerings. Every piece is of such practical utility and also of superior quality and beauty that we believe all will sell equally well. *They will certainly bring 50 cents each if you choose to ask it.*

THE ASSORTMENT COMPRISES 1-2 DOZEN EACH OF THE FOLLOWING:

High 6-Inch Footed Bowls with Overhanging 7-Inch Covers—Never surpassed in quality
Deep Scalloped Dishes—8½ inches in diameter. Consider the size and price.
Heavy Covered Dishes—7-inch with 8-inch overhanging cover. Extremely rich pattern.
Bread or Cake Trays—15 inches long, 6 inches wide, with silvered, high arch movable handle.

......Order here.   (*Total of 2 doz. to package. Sold only by package.*)   Price, $1.75 Doz.

Butler Brothers catalog, 1889

26

4 IN. CUMPORT

9 IN. SALVER

TUMBLER

GOBLET CUP FOOT

8 IN. COMPORT
WITH OR WITHOUT COVER

SPOON

1/2 GALL. PITCHER

Wallace & Company catalog, 1888

Pieces to be found in Starred Block include Covered Butter, Covered Sugar, Cream Pitcher, Spoon Holder, 1/2 Gallon Tankard Jug, Qt. Tankard Jug, Celery Vase, Goblet, Tumbler, Water Set, Lemonade Set, Berry Set, Salt, Pepper, Molasses Can, 10" Salver, 15" long and 6" wide Bread Tray W/ Metal Handle, 4" Comport, 5" Comport, 6" Comport, 7" Comport, 8" Comport, 5" Covered Comport, 6" Covered Comport, 7" Covered Comport, 8" Covered Comport, 5" Covered Bowl, 6" Covered Bowl, 7" Covered Bowl, 8" Covered Bowl, 5" Bowl, 6" Bowl, 7" Bowl, and an 8" Bowl.

Pattern No. 23D,
a.k.a. Quaker Lady

The Quaker Lady pattern was made in the late 1880s. It was probably first made in Wellsburg and continued at Findlay because of its immense popularity. It is a design of straight lines and simple crossed lines in the base. The lids also have droplets around the rims and are usually found damaged.

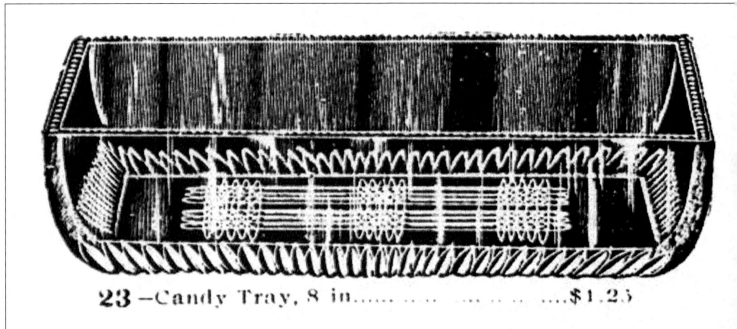

23 —Candy Tray, 8 in..................................$1.25

Ogden, Merrill & Greer catalog, 1895

Quaker Lady Tankard Pitcher, engraved, 13" high, 5 3/4" wide, $140-175.

Quaker Lady Bowl, 3 1/4" high, 8" wide, $50-65.
Quaker Lady Berry Bowl, small, 2" high, 4" wide, $25-30.
Quaker Lady Bowl, 3" high, 6" wide, $45-50.

Quaker Lady Tumbler, 3 7/8" high, 3" wide, $50-75.
Quaker Lady Goblet, engraved, 6 1/4" high, 3" wide, $55-80.

Quaker Lady Covered Compote, 10 1/2" high, 6 1/8" wide, $85-95.
Quaker Lady Covered Compote, $85-100.

Quaker Lady Spoon Holder, 4 3/4" high, 3 3/4" wide, $60-70.
Quaker Lady Celery, 6" high, 4 1/2" wide, $70-95.
Quaker Lady Covered Butter, 5 1/2" high, 6" wide base, 5 1/4" wide cover, $125-150.
Quaker Lady Covered Sugar, 6 1/4" high, 4 1/4" wide, $65-80.
Quaker Lady Cream Pitcher, 6 1/2" high, 3 3/4" wide, $55-65.

Quaker Lady Butter Dish showing the fragile lid. Note that the droplets on the lid get broken easily, making it difficult to find one in perfect condition.

Items of this pattern include Covered Butter, Covered Sugar, Cream Pitcher, Spoon Holder, 1/2 Gallon Jug, Goblet, Tumbler, Celery Vase, Cake Salver, Bowls of 5", 7", and 9", Open Comport of 8", 6" x 8" Candy Dish, 5" x 7" Candy Dish, and probably others. The plain parts of this pattern can be found engraved.

Pattern #25D,

a.k.a.

Ring and Swirl

The #25D pattern is known to collectors as Ring and Swirl. It is a beautiful pattern that evidently was not too well received by the public, as it is not too plentiful today.

Donaldson, Ogden & Co. catalog, 1893

Ring and Swirl Covered Compote, footed, $60-80.

Ring and Swirl Water Pitcher, $65-85.

Ring and Swirl Cup, $35-40.
Ring and Swirl Compote, high standard, $60-80.

Ring and Swirl Salt and Pepper Shakers, $85-120.

Known items in this pattern include Covered Butter, Covered Sugar, Spoon Holder, Cream Pitcher, Celery Vase, 1/2 Gallon Water Jug, Salt & Pepper Shakers, Goblet, Cake Salver, and Bread Tray.

Pattern # 28d Short Swirl

The No. 28D pattern was a short line and the only pieces known are the water pitcher and goblet. It is a simple but beautiful pattern.

Donaldson, Ogden & Co. catalog, 1893

28   Goblet

Ring and Swirl Goblet, 6" high, 2 7/8" wide, $30-45.

Short Swirl Goblet, 6" high, 2 7/8" wide, $30-45.

Onyx and Floradine

In the *Crockery and Glass Journal* dated December 6, 1888, an article appeared telling that: *some beautiful ware in crystal and rich colors is now being blown at the Dalzell, Gilmore & Leighton Co.'s works, and molds are being made for new patterns that will prove eye-openers. Some new colors are being produced that are very effective and attractive. This company is full of business, and is kept hustling to fill its orders.*

An interesting notice was posted in the *Crockery & Glass Journal* of January 10, 1889. *It having come to our knowledge that a pair of snaps of new design have been stolen from our works, we therefore warn all interested that we have applied for letters-patent to cover same. Yours Truly, Dalzell, Gilmore & Leighton Co.*

The previous information about the colors, new molds, and the missing tools were evidently the first information about the Oriental wares of Onyx and Floradine. This also describes the Autumn Leaf color, which was made for the many lampshades and globes. These shades and globes were also made in several colors of opalescent. This information was gathered from the handbook of George Leighton, which describes his experiments in colors.

Shards of Onyx and Floradine found at the factory site. Many color variations were found due to continual experimentation for the entire production time.

Pottery & Glassware Reporter, February 1889

The manufacture of the finest of glassware and the name Leighton have gone hand in hand through the history of glass making in the United States.

In 1848, Thomas Leighton, Sr. and his son William Leighton, Sr. developed a formula for ruby glass, the first formula for ruby glass in America. William Leighton, Sr. was a chemist and he imparted his knowledge to his son, William Leighton, Jr. and he to his son George Leighton. The chemist was probably the most valuable asset to a glass works. The manufacture of color ware and their formulas were closely guarded secrets.

The Leightons were responsible for many innovations in the production of glassware. Credited to them is the development of clear lime glass, Wheeling Peachblow, spangled ware, crimping devices, the Blackberry pattern and others including Onyx and Floradine.

When William, Jr., and his son George, became associated with Dalzell, Gilmore and Leighton at Findlay, Ohio, George registered a patent for a process, which produced Onyx and Floradine. The secret in bringing out the final colors in the heat sensitive glass was the reheating and exposure to either sulfur gas flame or sulfur gas fumes. Although the sulfur gas treatment was mentioned in the patent, no mention is found of it in the George Leighton handbook, which was a diary of his experiments.

In an attempt to bring some sense of reasoning into the distinction between Onyx and Floradine, let us examine the writings of the representative of the trade journal *Pottery and Glassware Reporter* as he observed this glassware for the first showing and questioned the salesman on duty at room 176 of the Monongahala House, Mr. E. D. Gilmore. – *What we want to call special attention to are their new lines of colored ware. The first of them, which they call 'Floradine' ware, is in two colors, ruby and autumn leaf, with the patterns elegantly traced on the exterior. The effect is extremely rich. In this they make sets, bottles, jugs, celeries, molasses cans, finger bowls, sugar dusters, shaker salts and peppers, mustards, toothpicks, 4" nappies, 8" bowls,*

and several other articles. The other, the 'Onyx' ware, is still more beautiful and there is nothing in glass on the market to surpass it. The colors of this are onyx, bronze and ruby and the pieces are all white lined. Like the 'Floradine', the pattern is impressed on the exterior in graceful forms, and only for the shining surface the ware would look more like fine china than glass. Of this they have now ready creams, sugars, half-gallon jugs, molasses cans and celeries—The above firm have the exclusive right to make these goods being the originators of them and have their privileges secured by patents.—

Although this is a quote from the year 1889, it is much more reliable than any guesswork that would be made today.

Floradine is found in a solid color, or sometimes a crystal with a thin color plating on the inside that gives the appearance of being a solid, or sometimes crystal with a surface color caused by the reheating process, this being borne out after careful study made of shards found at the factory site. By the above standards, it also can be found with either a satin finish or a glossy finish. Floradine colors include ruby, black, bronze, and green. The black, bronze, and green have been seen in glossy only. Shards of these colors have several layers of glass.

Using the before mentioned description, it appears that to be called Onyx the item must have the white lining or casing. Since this was the original display in January of 1889, it is possible that other items and colors were made later in each line. This has been previously presumed because of shards found at the factory site. It is believable that both wares were made with the same molds, as the cost of making separate molds would be prohibitive when the patterns are identical. The George Leighton handbook now confirms this.

Many guesses have been made about the near bankruptcy of this company because of the many problems in the manufacturing process of this beautiful glassware. Some reports were that the glass was too fragile and would shatter in your hand while holding it, but there is no proof that this actually happened. The fact is that not only the Onyx and Floradine, but also the Autumn Leaf and Rainbow colors would crack easily when producing the experiments while trying to find the best colors. This problem was solved by adding nitrate to the color batches and working the glass hot. We do know that moulds were expensive to make and that in the nearly nine months of manufacture that at least three different moulds were in existence for the sugar shaker alone. This is determined by the variations in the pattern. The report that Onyx and Floradine were produced for nine months is probably inaccurate, because George Leighton was still experimenting on this ware up until June of 1889. A lot of the different colors were made from the experimental batches and are on the market as production pieces.

It must be noted that although it has been written many times that bankruptcy was near, it is difficult to believe because of the enormous trade that this firm enjoyed in lamp production. To understand this reasoning, let us look at an article that appeared in *The Pottery and Glassware Reporter* dated July 18,1889: *Dalzell, Gilmore & Leighton Co. hold out at Room 135,with E. D. Gilmore in charge – The 'Royal Arch' lamp, with black base and Floradine bowl, is a very tasteful article, and the 'Daisy,' also with a black base and Floradine bowl, is a pretty specimen too. They have a new line of crystal ware, No. 33, sets, bowls, etc., and show this in plain crystal and stained. There is a line of crystal and colored gas globes and 10 and 14 inch domes and they have a big layout of miscellaneous wares.*

Another factor that must also be considered is the formula for the white plating that was used inside the Onyx and the effect that it had on the pots. Recorded in the Leighton handbook is the formula, which had also been used to plate Amberina to make the Hobbs Coral ware. It had been noted that this formula had an adverse effect upon the pots. This problem was resolved by changing the production to a continuous tank furnace.

On August 1, 1889, it was noted that the company had started running a small tank furnace for their fancy colored ware, saving a large sum in broken pots. This also lends to the theory that costly problems were in the manufacture and not in the breakage of the glass.

One of the most overlooked problems in the manufacture of this glassware has been brought forward by serious collectors, and was probably the most costly for the company. The first and foremost reason for the manufacture of any product is profit. If the merchandise is too costly to make then there is no profit.

When looking at many shards of Onyx it appears that many colors were produced. In reality there was a problem in getting the correct mix in the batch. According to the George Leighton handbook, he would continuously change the formula until the color was what he wanted. He had struck several pieces in a *bad* color and then tried a different mix. Contrary to popular belief, the color never varied by the amount of heat when reheating to bring the color out. Every piece made from a batch would have the same color when finished. For example the first try at ruby red turned out a rose color.

The Floradine glass did not escape the same problems, as different shades of red are found. Leighton started his experiments for the Floradine red about December 13, 1888, and had it perfected a few days later. Of course this was not the same formula as the red used in Onyx because it was not heat sensitive. The first experimental batch for red came out an orange red, which Leighton called a bad color.

Part of the manufacturing process sometimes employed was the use of a finishing mold with a smooth surface. With the glass reheated, this mold would cause the leaves and flowers to be impressed into the item and can be detected by the amount of relief on the inside.

This presents no problem with the pattern or the values, but it does cause some slight variations as to the distinctness of the pattern. The temperature of the glass when this process was used determined the sharpness of the pattern.

Some items of Onyx have been found recently that have had foreign substances applied to the outer surface. This was evidently done for the sole purpose of trying to mislead collectors and gain a higher price. The perpetrator didn't know that there were no painted surfaces on this ware. The colors are the glass itself. One piece was a sugar shaker that had been painted blue. Another piece, a toothpick holder, has been found that had been broken, glued back together, and then painted a bronze color.

The Water Bottle

Among the items that have been found is a water bottle of which an explanation is not known. It has the Onyx white surface with platinum flowers and leaves but is then plated with a clear glass with the Consolidated Lamp & Glass Co.'s Florette pattern impressed in the outer surface. Where this was done and who did it is unknown. There are five known examples of this item.

George Leighton

George Leighton, the originator of the formula for this beautiful glass, graduated from Harvard with a degree in chemistry and immediately became one of the original partners of Dalzell, Gilmore and Leighton. When the limited production of Onyx and Floradine was halted about eight months after its start, George remained a partner but left the glass business. He left Findlay, Ohio, and moved to Chicago, Illinois. He then attended Northwestern University Law School and was admitted to the Illinois Bar in 1893. The rest of his professional life he specialized in real estate law. He died April 25, 1945, at his home in Hinsdale, Illinois. He was eighty-one years of age. He was buried at Sleepy Hollow Cemetery in Concord, Massachusetts.

Floradine Cream Pitcher, Rose color, satin finish, 4 1/2" high, 2 5/8" wide, $1,400-$1,550.
Floradine Cream Pitcher, Cinnamon color, satin finish, $1,300-$1,400.

Floradine Spoon Holder, cranberry, glossy finish, 4 1/2" high, 2 1/4" wide, $1,000-$1,200.

Floradine Pickle Castor, cranberry, satin finish, $6,000-$8,000.

Floradine Spoon Holder, cranberry opalescent, glossy, 4 1/2" high, 2 1/4" wide, $300-$400.

Floradine Spoon Holder, black, glossy, 4 1/2" high, 2 1/4" wide, $3,500-$4,500.

Onyx Toothpick Holder, platinum, 2 3/8" high, 2 3/8" wide, $625+.
Floradine Toothpick Holder, satin finish, 2 1/2" high, 2" wide, $1,700-$1,800.

Floradine Mustard Pot, satin finish, nickel plated top, 3 1/2" high to top of lid, $2,000-$2,200.

Onyx Water Pitcher, silver, 8" high, $550-750.

Onyx Spoon Holder, 4 1/2" high, 2 1/4" wide, $350-400.
Onyx Celery, 6 1/4" high, 3 1/8" wide, $350-400.
Onyx Vase, 3 3/4" high, 2 1/8" wide, $400-450.

Onyx Covered Butter, $450-600.

Onyx Cream Pitcher, 4 1/2" high, 2 1/4" wide, $375-500.
Onyx Spoon Holder, 4 1/2" high, 2 1/4" wide, $350-400.

Onyx Celery, bronze, 6 1/4" high, 3 1/8" wide, $350-450.

Onyx Sugar Shaker, rose
flowers, 5" high, $1,500+.

Onyx Celery, purple flowers, 6 1/4" high, 3 1/8" wide, the purple color has flowed on the body of the piece, $4,500-$5,000.

Onyx Tumbler, purple flowers, 3 1/2" high, 2 3/4" wide, $3,000-3,500.

Daisy Lamp, Onyx font with black base, $ 7,000+.
This lamp is too rare to place an absolute value. This is the only one reported.

Royal Arch Lamp, a.k.a. Onyx Two Post Lamp, Black Two Post base with Onyx font. Note the difference in the font in this lamp and the Daisy Lamp, $18,000+.
This lamp is also too rare to value with any degree of certainty as these lamps are very seldom on the market.

Onyx Cream Pitcher, bronze, 4 1/2"
high 2 5/8" wide, $450-600.

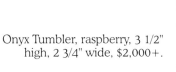

Onyx Tumbler, raspberry, 3 1/2"
high, 2 3/4" wide, $2,000+.

Onyx Spoon Holder, bronze, 4 1/2"
high, 2 1/4" wide, $450-600.

Floradine Mustard, 3 1/2" high, $2,000+.
Onyx Mustard, 3 1/2" high, $500+.

Onyx Covered Sugar, raspberry,
the color of the flowers bled
into the white base color,
$2,000+.

Onyx Berry Bowl, 1 3/4" high, 4 1/8" wide, $200-250.
Onyx Finger Bowl, 2 1/2" high, 4 1/8" wide, $300-350.

Onyx Celery, cinnamon tint to flowers, $2,000+.

Onyx Syrup, silver, $1,500+.

Floradine Cream Pitcher, $2,000+.
Floradine Sugar, covered, $2,000+.

Onyx Water Pitcher and Tumblers, Tumblers are the half pattern, $1,200+.

Floradine Cream Pitcher, glossy, $1,400+.

Floradine Cream Pitcher, cinnamon, satin finish, $1,400+.

Onyx Sugar Shaker, raspberry, $1,800+.

Floradine Covered Butter, cranberry satin finish, $1,800+.

Floradine Celery, cranberry, satin finish, $2,500+.
Old tag with price and place of purchase on the bottom.

Floradine Tumbler, satin finish, 3/4 surface pattern, $1,300+.

Floradine Mustard, cinnamon, satin finish, $2,000+.

Onyx Salt and Pepper Shakers in silver-plated holder, $1,000+.

Floradine Syrup, raspberry, $4,500+.

Onyx Water Pitcher, bronze, $6,000+.

Onyx Butter Base, bronze, $350+.

Onyx Pickle Castor, $3,500+.

Onyx Water Pitcher, cranberry, amber handle, $6,500+.

Onyx Syrup, this is one of the early colors of a red-orange and the color bled into the white base color. It ended as a beautiful piece, $3,500+.

Onyx Tumble Up, Water Bottle and straight side Tumbler. This is described in the text. There are five such accounted for, $2,200+.

Floradine Tumbler, glossy, full pattern, $1,200+.

Floradine Tumbler, satin, three quarter pattern, 1,200+.

Onyx Tumbler, raspberry, half pattern, $2,200+.

Onyx Tumbler, straight side, silver, used with the Tumble Up Set, $600+.

Onyx Tumbler, silver, three quarter pattern, $400+.

Onyx Tumbler, red to orange, half pattern, $2,200+.

Floradine Lid, raspberry, 6 1/2" diameter. A base has not been found that it will fit. It is not the shape of a butter lid and is larger than the butter base.

Pattern #35D, a.k.a. Diagonal Block with Thumbprint

3114 Catsup.

Wallace & Company catalog

Diagonal Block with Thumbprint Goblet, $40-65.

This pattern was introduced in 1889 and consisted of only three known items, the Half Gallon Squat Water Jug, Tumbler, and a Catsup Bottle. There are probably other forms to be found. It has been found in clear glass only.

Diagonal Block with Thumbprint Syrup, $110-135.

Diagonal Block with Thumbprint Cruet, $85-110.
Diagonal Block with Thumbprint Tumbler, $50-65.

Puritan Pattern

The 1889 Dalzell, Gilmore and Leighton illustrated advertisement also included the Puritan Tankard Water Pitcher. The Water Pitcher in this pattern was available in several varieties. The illustration shown here has a rayed base. It also came in a *Kaleidoscope* base, as did all the other pieces. The 1/2 Gallon Pitchers were also made in a Squat type.

The items in this pattern include the two 1/2 Gallon Tankards mentioned, squat 1/2 Gallon Pitcher, Milk Pitcher, Cream Pitcher, Covered Butter, Covered Sugar, Spoon Holder, Tumbler, and Celery Vase. Comports and other items may have been made. As with most patterns, this pattern was available with engravings. This pattern has been found in clear glass only.

Puritan, engraved..................................$5.00
        "   plain...................................3.60
Lowest priced plain polished tankard.

Ogden, Merrill & Greer catalog, 1895

Puritan Tankard Pitcher, engraved, $85-135.

Novelties

Following are excerpts of articles from *China, Glass & Lamps*. *11-18-91: Among the elegant novelties just got out is the 'Amour' jug, of a most graceful and artistic shape, with handsome metallic handle, connected with the jug by two bands, finished in the most ornate manner. This is an article that is sure to have a big sale. The 'Bugle' decanter is another new thing got out by the firm, and it is going to have its place too.*

7-12-91: The company are showing several new additions to their line of seasonal novelties, the 'Arragon' plate being particularly noticeable. The glass made by this firm is clear as crystal and they never had a better run of it than last season.

7-14-91: Among novelties, Mr. and Mrs. Snowball and their children—Dase and Snowball, Jr. – are great favorites and sell like hot cakes. Their popularity has induced the firm to produce other figures, a sailor, clown, German—the latter two both plain and decorated—and there is a great demand for them. There is a wine in the shape of a parrot, with bronzed head and feet, pipes, daggers, etc., for use as flasks or confectionery, and an ingenious device for desk purposes, useful for holding rubber stamps or other things. On the whole this is a notable display.

7-20-92: We might further mention another novelty just got out by this firm. It is a campaign flask with etched mirror inserted in one side, showing what any beholder must naturally consider the best two men of his party.

7-12-93: The company are showing several new additions to their line of seasonal novelties, the 'Arragon' plate being particularly noticeable.

1-23-95: Dalzell, Gilmore & Leighton Co. have just sent to Mr. Lambie samples of fresh novelties in the way of salts that will be wonderful sellers, or we miss our guess. The boys at the factory dubbed them 'the euchre set,' as they are made in heart, diamond, and club shapes, with a four spot and five spot of an odd suit. The little things are beautifully finished, and sparkle like diamonds. Every buyer who has seen them included several gross in his order.

The No. 66D, a.k.a. Floral Fence, plate was made as a plate and also with a metal frame and handle making a basket.

Other novelties include a Sheaf Toothpick, Brush Pickle, Skillet Nappy, Thistle Pickle, and a Hand Nappy. The molds for these novelties were sent to National's No. 9 Glass Works at Greentown, Indiana, where for many years they were thought to have originated.

Mrs. Snowball
And Other Novelties

It was announced on July 18, 1889, that: *The celebrated "Snowball" is on deck yet and they are getting out a wench to bear him company.*

Mrs. Snowball was illustrated in an advertisement in the *Crockery & Glass Journal* dated October 16, 1890. In the same advertisement the Snowball Wine Set and the Old German Pipe Flask, with Amber Mouth Piece, are shown.

The *Crockery & Glass Journal* of October 23, 1890, carried a Dalzell, Gilmore & Leighton illustrated advertisement showing the German Gentleman Decanter, Clown Decanter, Dagger Cologne, and the No. 130 and No. 131 colognes.

An illustrated advertisement in *China, Glass & Lamps* displayed the No. 39D Berry Set; but most important were two more novelties, the No. 1 Stamp Rack that has an Owl atop and the Parrot Decanter.

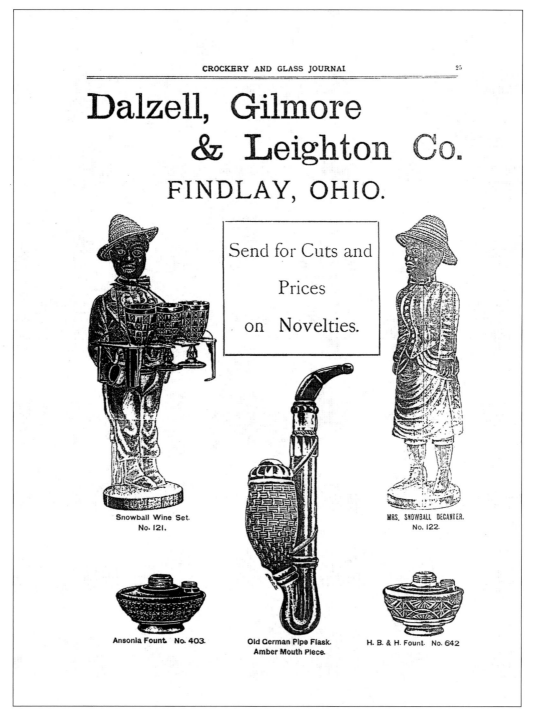

Crockery & Glass Journal, October 16, 1890

It was written in *China, Glass and Lamps,* dated November 18, 1891, that: *Dalzell, Gilmore & Leighton – Among the elegant novelties just got out is the "Amour" jug, of a most graceful and artistic shape, with handsome metallic handle, connected to the jug by two bands, finished in the most ornate manner. – The "Bugle" decanter is another new thing got out by the firm.*

The Dalzell, Gilmore & Leighton catalog of 1895 also illustrates novelties of six assorted Euchre Individual salts, six sizes of Genoese (Eyewinker) Colognes which are called Rainey Ball by collectors, a small Lantern Shaped Salt, Hand Nappy, Skillet Nappy, Thistle Pickle, Brush Pickle, and Sheaf Toothpick Holder (the last five items having previously attributed to the National Glass Company at their Greentown, Indiana, glass works.

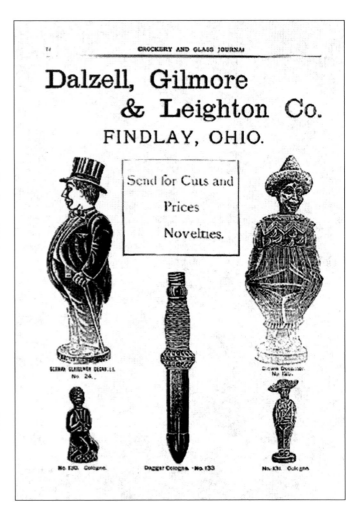

Crockery & Glass Journal,
October 23, 1890

China, Glass & Lamps, February 18, 1891

Mr. Snowball has a frosted black glass head with traces of original paint (eyes, lips, and teeth originally were painted). Body of Mr. Snowball is clear glass frosted. 14" high, $700-900.

Clown Decanter has white milk glass head with original paint. Body of the clown is clear frosted glass. 12 3/4" high, $700-1,000.

Mr. Snowball is with original brass tray and hat. The cordial glasses are clear. 13 1/2" high, $1,200-1,500.

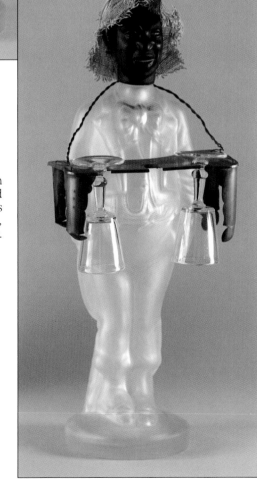

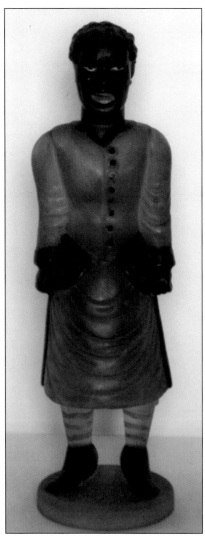

Mrs. Snowball has a black glass head frosted with original paint. Body of Mrs. Snowball is clear frosted with much of the original black paint intact. Her blouse and skirt show little of the original red paint. Stockings are frosted and have rings of gray paint. 13 1/2" high, $1,200-1,400.

German Gentleman, decanter, has a white milk glass head with original paint. Body is clear frosted glass with most all of the original paint. 12 1/2" high, $900-1,000.

German Gentleman with a reproduction hat made just for him by his present owner, $900-1,000.

68

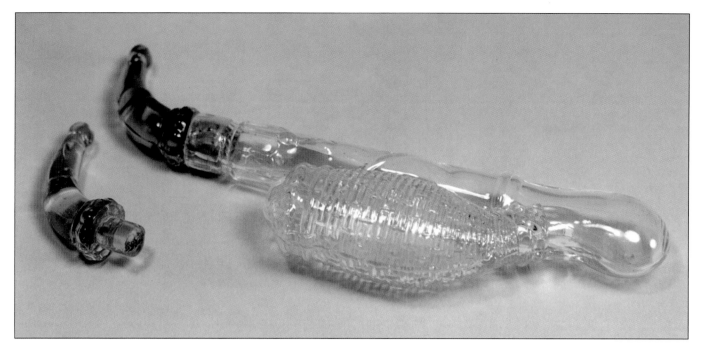

Old German pipe flask, clear with amber mouthpiece, 8 1/2" long, mouthpiece 3 1/8" long, $100-150 complete.
Green mouthpiece, $35-50.

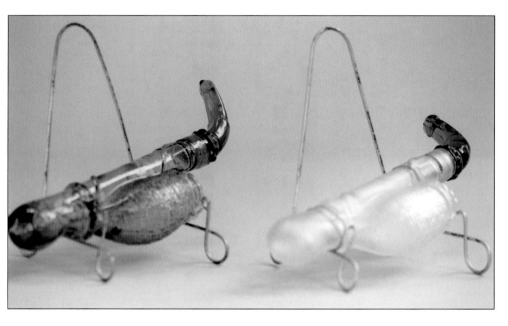

Pipe bottle, amber with amber mouthpiece, 8 1/2" long, mouthpiece 3 1/8" long, $175-225.
Pipe bottle, clear, frosted, with amber mouthpiece, 8 1/2" long, mouthpiece 3 1/8" long, $135-195. The pipe bottle was made for retail sale and offered to other manufacturers in which to package their products (e.g. candy container).

Dagger Cologne, original tin lid, 11" long, $135-175.

Campaign Flask, all original, clear, Daisy and Button pattern on one side. Other side has beaded oval with glued on mirror. Lid is made of tin. 5 1/2" high, $400-600.

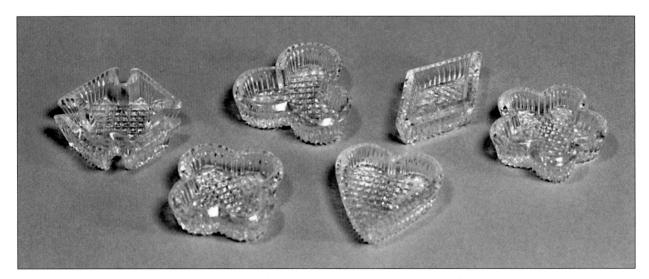

Euchre saltcellars were made in 6 shapes. (Measurements are from the widest point.)
  a) Maltese Cross. 7/16" high, 1 5/8" wide, $15-25.
  b) 4 Lobe. 7/16" high, 1 3/16" wide, $15-25.
  c) 3 Lobe 7/16" high, 1 3/4" wide, $15-25.
  d) Heart 7/16" high, 1 1/2" long, $20-35.
  e) Diamond. 7/16" high, 2" wide, $20-30.
  f) 5 Lobe 7/16" high, 1 3/4" wide, $15-20.

Parrot decanter has a glass body with pewter head and feet that were originally silver-plated. The glass eyes are the same glass eyes as found in Teddy Bears of the period. Parrot, blue-green with yellow eyes, 9 1/8" high, $600-900.

Boxer Bottle, a.k.a. Fitzsimmons bottle, the upper torso is made of an opaque lavender color of glass. This part of the bottle is removable. Base is clear frosted glass with painted leggings and shoes. 14 1/2" high, $1,200-1,600.

Parrot decanter has a glass body with pewter head and feet that were originally silver-plated. The glass eyes are the same glass eyes as found in Teddy Bears of the period. Parrot, Vaseline color with red eyes, 9 1/8" high, $600-900.

Parrot decanter has a glass body with pewter head and feet that were originally silver-plated. The glass eyes are the same glass eyes as found in Teddy Bears of the period. Parrot, blue with the yellow eyes, 9 1/8" high, $600-900.

Parrot decanter, head with yellow eyes.

Parrot decanter, head with red eyes.

66D Floral Fence, Plate, clear, 10", $60-80.

66D Floral Fence, Plate, amber, 10", $80-100.

66D Floral Fence, Plate, blue, 10", $95-125.

66D Floral Fence, Plate, Clear, frosted, 10", $80-110.

Skillet Nappy, 6" diameter, 7 7/8" long, $40-50.
The National Glass Company at the Indiana Goblet and Tumbler
Company later made the Skillet and named it Connecticut
Skillet. The original mold was used.

Sheaf Toothpick Holder, blue, 3" high,
1 1/3" wide, $225+.
Sheaf Toothpick Holder, clear, 3" high,
1 1/3" wide, $95+.
Sheaf Toothpick Holder, amber, 3"
high, 1 1/3" wide, $150+.
This mold was transferred to the
Indiana Goblet and Tumbler Company. The amber was possibly made
there. The St. Clair Company has
reproduced this Toothpick Holder.

Brush Pickle, 8" long, $50-60. The hairbrush was only produced in clear glass at Findlay, Ohio.
The National Glass Company at the Indiana Goblet and Tumbler Company later made the Brush.

Thistle Pickle, 8" long, $60-75.
The Thistle pickle was produced only in clear glass at Findlay. This is another of the molds that was sent to the
Indiana Tumbler and Goblet Co. in Indiana. It was reproduced from the original mold and named Scotch Thistle.

Mitted Hand, 2 7/8" high, 6" wide. The mold for this pattern was sent to
the Indiana Goblet and Tumbler Co. and reproduced there, $35-45.

Star and Feather
Plate, $85.

Inverted Hobnail Arches
Mug, $50.

Pattern 37D La Grippe, a.k.a. Convex Rib

Early illustrations of this pattern in the trade journals show the name to be La Grippe. The earliest illustrations appeared in 1889. Items made include Covered Butter, Covered Sugar, Cream Pitcher, Spoon Holder, Rose Bowl, 5" Compotes – both open and covered, Half Gallon Tankard Pitcher, Half Gallon Squat Pitcher, Goblet, Tumbler, and a Berry Set.

37 Half-gallon Squat Pitcher

G. Sommers & Company catalog, 1892

La Grippe Berry Set, $140-165.

La Grippe Fruit Bowl, ruffle edge, $65-85.
La Grippe Bowl, flat, $35-45.

81

Pattern 39D, a.k.a.
Big Diamond, a.k.a. Arkansas

Two new patterns were introduced in 1890 and first produced in 1891. The trade journal *China, Glass and Lamps* contained an article in their January 14, 1891, issue that tells us: *Dalzell, Gilmore and Leighton Co., of Findlay, O., are displaying a beautiful line of samples in Room 156. They are in charge of Mr. James Dalzell of the firm. Their new pattern, 'Magnolia,' is one of the hits of the season. This is an etched design with the beautiful flower of the South showing in crystal. The shapes are tasteful and we have never seen prettier pitchers. They have a full line of this and the dealers will want to get it. No. 39 is another new pattern—and a nice one too. —'The Silver Leaf' is a beautiful ware and continues its hold on the trade. They have an elegant line of tankard pitchers, goblets, tumblers, and other goods.*

G. Sommers & Co. catalog, 1892

The Big Diamond pattern was introduced in December of 1890 and production was ongoing in January of 1891. It was somewhat limited in the number of different pieces made in comparison to the other patterns. Items known to exist in this pattern include: A Covered Butter, Covered Sugar, Cream Pitcher, Spoon

Holder, Celery Vase, Pickle Dish, Cake Salver, 8" Comport, 8" High Standard Bowl, 4 1/2" Nappy, and a 1/2 Gallon Pitcher. It has been found only in clear glass.

Big Diamond Tumbler, $65-85.

Pattern 41D Magnolia

The Magnolia pattern was introduced at the same time as was Big Diamond, a.k.a. Arkansas. It was sold in either clear or with the figures frosted. The frosted effect makes a most beautiful show. The known items in this pattern include the Covered Butter, Cream Pitcher, Spoon Holder, Covered Sugar, 9" Cake Salver, Celery Vase, 4" Comport, 6" Comport, 7" Comport, 8" Comport, Blown Syrup, Pressed Syrup, Salt, Pepper, 1/2 Gallon Water Jug, Goblet, and Tumbler.

Patterns of 1892
The company always had their mold shop busy and molds for the year of 1892 kept the mold shop at work as new patterns were to be introduced in December of 1891. Two of the patterns would be ready

by January but two others that had been planned would not have the molds completed until a month or so later. The original report in *China, Glass & Lamps* is: *The year just now closing has been a prosperous one with Dalzell, Gilmore & Leighton Co., and they have done an excellent trade, running three furnaces and a tank all the time. They look for a good trade also in the coming season. To meet all the wants of the trade they have got ready four new patterns, which will fill the bill in every particular. 43 D is a low priced line, but withall a neat and tasteful pattern, and is well worth what is asked for it. 47 D is another handsome line, offered at a very moderate cost and it is bound to make the riffle. 45 and 49 D are the other two lines and they are of novel design and altogether out of the common run of such things. There are full lines of each of these patterns, of which we shall give a more detailed account in a future issue, and we can confidently recommend them to the notice of the trade. Dalzell, Gilmore & Leighton Co. have made a big record in the glassware line and they, as well as others, think they beat previous successes in their present effort.*

The *Crockery & Glass Journal* of December 31, 1891 records: *The Dalzell, Gilmore & Leighton Co. come to the front with an early announcement of their Four New Lines, which they are now ready to show as trade makers for 1892. If you will cast your eye over the page of particulars you will see that they have given you a complete list of the four lines, which they fully expect will keep them busy throughout the year and run their three furnaces and tanks continuously. Their Mr. James Dalzell will open up at the Monongahela House in Pittsburgh on January 4th, and remain there until February 20th, with a full line of samples; and he invites all dealers arriving in Pittsburgh during that period to call and see what he has to offer in the new lines.*

China, Glass & Lamps, February 1891

Magnolia Water Pitcher, clear, $75-100.
Magnolia Water Pitcher, frosted, $125-195.
Frosted Magnolia was produced in clear and with frosted design. Frosted is more desirable than the clear. A complete table set was produced plus bowls. No covered compotes have been seen.

Magnolia Syrup, frosted, 6 1/2" high to top of lid, flat base 3 1/4", $125-$175. Magnolia Syrup, frosted, 8" high to top of lid, 3" collar base, $150-$225. Magnolia Syrup, clear, 8" high to top of tin lid, 3" collar base, $95-$150.

Magnolia Salt Shaker, 2 1/4" high, $75-$100.

Magnolia Goblet, 6" high and 3 1/4" wide, $75-$95.

Magnolia Sugar, covered, frosted, $85-150.
Magnolia, Celery, 5 3/4" high, $85-$150.
Magnolia, Cream Pitcher, 5" to top of spout, $75-$125.

Magnolia Cake Salver, frosted, $125-$175.

Pattern 43D, a.k.a. Teardrop

One of the first to be produced of the four new patterns was the No. 43D. Don Smith called this pattern Teardrop. It is so similar to the 45D pattern that some of the pieces could be interchangeable. We are listing them as we think Don would have.

The Teardrop pattern has been found in clear glass only in the Covered Butter, Covered Sugar, Spoon Holder, Cream Pitcher, a Berry Set, Half-gallon Water Jug, and a Tumbler.

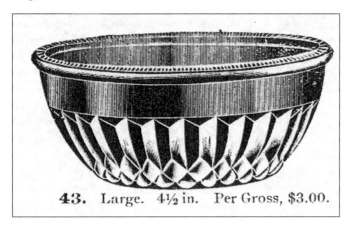

Ogden, Merrill and Company catalog, 1895

Dewdrop and Fan Goblet, $65-85.

Pattern 44D, a.k.a. Dewdrop and Fan, a.k.a. Fantop Hobnail

Very few items have been reported in this pattern. Known items are the Goblet and Berry Set.

Butler Brothers, 1894

Pattern 45D, a.k.a. Teardrop Clear

The Teardrop Clear pattern is a similar pattern to Teardrop. As with the Teardrop pattern there was not a full line. Evidently neither pattern proved to be popular, therefore it is not easy to find today.

G. Sommers & Company catalog, 1894

The illustrated Tankard Pitcher was identified by pattern number in the catalog. If not for this identification it would hardly be known to be a part of this pattern. Some of the pieces of this pattern have only the upper bars and the teardrops. This pattern has been confused with the Teardrop pattern, but close examination will illustrate the difference. It is found in clear but could possibly exist in emerald green. Known items include the Covered Butter, Covered Sugar, Cream Pitcher, Spoon Holder, Open Compotes, Tankard Water Pitcher, Squat Water Pitcher, and Tumbler. The Tankard Pitcher has a version of the pattern, which closely resembles the Pittsburg pattern made by Bryce Brothers. This explains the mistaken attribution of the Pittsburg pattern to Findlay. Finding a shard of a part of this pattern would cause a person to believe that it was the Pittsburg pattern.

Teardrop Clear Celery, $45-65.

Teardrop Clear Covered Compote, high standard, $95-135.

Teardrop Clear Open Compote, piecrust rim, $95-135.

Pattern #47D,
a.k.a. Swirl and Cable

This pattern was also introduced in 1892. It is a beautiful but elusive pattern. The list of items that were made is from an 1895 Dalzell. Gilmore and Leighton Company catalog. There are the Sugar and Cover, Butter and Cover, Cream, Spoon, 4" Nappy, 4 1/2" Nappy, 6" Nappy, 7" Nappy, 8" Nappy, 4" Hand Nappy, 6" Hand Nappy, 6" Nappy and Cover, 7" Nappy and Cover, 8" Nappy and Cover, 4 1/2" Jelly and Cover, 6" Bowl and Cover, 7" Bowl and Cover, 8" Bowl and Cover, 4 1/2" Jelly, 6" Bowl, 7" Bowl, 8" Bowl, Half-gallon Pitcher, Quart Pitcher, Pint Pitcher, 9" Salver, Tankard Cream, Goblet, Tumbler, Celery, Condiment Set, 6" Plate, 4-ounce Vinegar, Salt, Pepper, Straw Jar and Cover, Molasses Can, Tin Top, Molasses Can, Nickel Top, Mug, Water Set, Lemonade Set and Berry Set. As one can see this was an extensive pattern It has been found in clear glass only.

Swirl and Cable Goblet, 6" high, 3" wide, $35-$50. Swirl and Cable was made only in clear glass. A complete table set and other pieces were also made.

47. 4 in., Good Size, Per Gross, $2.75.

Ogden, Merrill & Greer catalog, 1895

Swirl and Cable Covered Compote, 11 1/4" high, 9" wide, $60-$95.
Swirl and Cable Jelly Compote, 7 3/4" high, 4 3/4" wide, $50-$60.
Swirl and Cable Open Compote, 6 3/4" high, 8" wide, $25-$40.

Swirl and Cable Pitcher, pint, $65-85.
Swirl and Cable Pitcher, 1/2 Gallon, $55-75.
Swirl and Cable Pitcher, quart, $65-85.

Pattern 49D, a.k.a. Bulls Eye and Diamond Point, a.k.a. Reverse Torpedo

This pattern is one of the most popular of this firm. The last of the four new patterns to be introduced in 1892, it has been found in clear only and with engraving and sometimes a piecrust edge. Items made are Sugar and Cover, Butter and Cover, Cream, Spoon, 4" Comport, 6" Comport, 7" Comport, 8" Comport, 6" Comport and Cover, 7" Comport and Cover, 8" Comport and Cover, 5" Jelly and Cover, 6" Bowl and Cover, 7" Bowl and Cover, 8" Bowl and Cover, 5" Jelly, 6" Bowl, 7" Bowl, 8" Bowl, Half-gallon Pitcher, Tumbler, Goblet, Celery, Honey and Cover, 6" Hand Nappy, Salt, Pepper, 10" Salver, Cracker Jar and Cover, Water Set, Lemonade Set, Berry Set, 6" Fruit Dish, 7" Fruit Dish, 8" Fruit Dish, 6" Fruit Bowl, 7" Fruit Bowl, 8" Fruit Bowl, Orange Stand, Salver Basket, and Bowl Basket.

Bulls Eye with Diamond Point Water Pitcher, engraved, 11 3/4" high, 4 1/4" wide, $125-175.
Usually found in clear. Has been found with a cut design and with red flashing but this is very rare.

DALZELL
Gilmore & Leighton
CO.,
Tableware.
Lamps.
Novelties.   FINDLAY, O.

China, Glass & Lamps, April 27, 1892

Bulls Eye with Diamond Point Honey Dish, 6" high, 6 1/2" wide, $125-150.

Bulls Eye with Diamond Point Goblet, 6" high, 3 1/8" wide, $40-75.

Bulls Eye with Diamond Point Salt and Pepper Shakers, 3" high, $65-85 pair.

Bulls Eye with Diamond Point Jelly Compote, covered, 7 1/8" high, 4 1/4" lid diameter, $95-125.

Bulls Eye with Diamond Point Spoon Holder, 5" high, 3 1/4" wide, $55-65.
Bulls Eye with Diamond Point Covered Sugar, 6 1/2" high, 3 5/8" wide, $50-85.
Bulls Eye with Diamond Point Covered Butter, 5 1/2" high, $50-85.
Bulls Eye with Diamond Point Celery, 6" high, $60-95.
Bulls Eye with Diamond Point Cream Pitcher, 6" high, 2 3/4" base, $65-85.

Bulls Eye with Diamond Point Novelty, 3" high, 4 1/2" wide, $50-75.
Ladies spittoon? It was made from the tumbler mold. Has a
ground base.

Bulls Eye with Diamond Point Bowl with Brass Handle, 3" high,
8 1/2" wide, $75-95. Bowl with original brass handle.

Bulls Eye with Diamond Point Tumbler (right), 3 3/4" high, 2 3/4" wide, $45-60.

Bulls Eye with Diamond Point Cake Stand, $135-200.

Genoese Pattern, a.k.a. Eyewinker

From the *China, Glass and Lamps* of January 11, 1893, we find the following information. *Dalzell, Gilmore & Leighton – This firm is represented by James Dalzell in room 156. The chief attraction among his samples is the new Genoese tableware pattern, which is unquestionably the most beautiful of the many elegant lines brought out by this firm and one which mere words cannot do adequate justice to. It comprises 60 pieces –* set, pitchers of several sizes, bonbon, salt, pepper, tumblers, goblets, covered bowls, comports, jelly and pickle jars, the same articles without covers, nappies, square top bowls, comports and jelly, catsup, syrup, nut bowls footed and without foot, nick nacks, confections, celery tray and bread tray. This is a line that no stock with any pretensions to elegance can afford to be without. The glass is clear as crystal and the designs are unique, handsome and original. They will have another plain pattern in a few days, to which no name has yet been given. It has a crimped edge, the crimping being done by a new method employed by this firm exclusively and it is a bright and brilliant pattern. The firm have put in an oil plant at the factory, which is now in operation. They worked during the holidays, but since had an enforced idleness of a week from insufficient supply of gas. Hereafter they expect to be able to run full.*

It should be pointed out that there are variations within this pattern. The most obvious is that several of the pieces are with the encapsulated balls at the base and the panels only. They don't have the eyes. These include most Lids, the Goblet, the Tumbler, and some Sauce Dishes. Some pieces in this pattern have a square rim while the majorities are round. The Cruets, known as Rainey Ball, are actually Genoese Colognes and were made in six different sizes. They were in 1 oz., 2 oz., 4 oz., 6 oz., 8 oz., and 12 oz. This pattern has been found in clear only. There are reproductions and mostly in color.

G. Sommers & Co., 1894

Genoese Sauce Dish, clear, 1 6/16" high, 4 1/8" diameter, $25-35.
NOTES: Goblet, a sauce, and tumblers all have same pattern variant.

Genoese Pitcher, clear, 9 1/2" high, 4 1/2" base diameter, $150-185.
(a.k.a.: Eyewinker Cannon Ball, Crystal Ball, Winking Eye). The old examples were made only in clear glass. The goblet, tumbler, cologne, most lids, and a sauce do not have the eye on them.

Genoese Goblet, clear, 5 3/4" high, 3" diameter, $60-95.

Genoese Syrup, clear, 6 1/8" to top of nickel-plated brass lid, $145-165.

Genoese Salt and Pepper Shakers, clear, 3" high, $95-125 pair.

Genoese Cake Salver, clear, 6 1/2" high, 9 1/4" diameter, $145-195.

Genoese Cologne, clear, 6 7/8" high, $135-150. These colognes were made in 1 oz., 2 oz., 4 oz., 6 oz., 8 oz., and 12 oz. sizes. All are difficult to find. Shown with the original stopper. Later, the ball stopper used with the Priscilla pattern was used. Probably there was too much breakage with the original one. Also was more economical to produce a piece that could be used with several patterns.

Genoese Pickle Caster, clear, 3 3/4" high, 3 1/8" wide pickle caster insert. 9" total height with silver-plated holder, $195-220.

Genoese Cream, clear, 6 3/4" high, $50-75.
Genoese Spoon Holder, clear, 5 1/4" high, $50-75.
Genoese Butter, covered, clear, 6 1/4" high, $55-80.
Genoese Celery, clear, 6 1/2" high, $65-80.
Genoese Sugar, covered, 6 1/2" high, $75-95.

Genoese Orange Stand, clear, $135-160.

Genoese Compotes, open, clear, $75-125.

Genoese Compotes, covered, clear, $85-145 ea.

Columbia Pattern

The *China, Glass & Lamps* trade journal of July 5, 1893, carried the following article. *Dalzell, Gilmore & Leighton Co. have run their tank and three furnaces full without any loss of time beyond their control during the entire fire, and got through the last turn on June 30 at midnight. Their sales have been largely increased over any previous year. On page 26 of this issue will be found illustrations of their new Columbia pattern, which is a large line, comprising sixty-two pieces. To be fully appreciated this pattern must be seen. It is the brightest they ever produced and is sure to be a good seller, as plain ware – provided it is graceful in design – is always in demand. The crimping, to which special attention is called, is done by machinery, thus insuring its uniformity. This crimping is sufficient to relieve the line from the monotony of extreme plainness and as a whole the pattern is all that could be desired.*

1895 catalog: Set, Sugar, Butter, Cream, Spoon, 3 1/2" Open Comport, 4" Open Comport, 5" Open Comport, 6" Open Comport, 7" Open Comport, 8" Open Comport, 3 1/2" Square Open Comport, 4" Square Open Comport, 5" Square Open Comport, 6" Square Open Comport, 7" Square Open Comport, 3 1/2" Crazy Edge Open Comport, 4" Crazy Edge Open Comport, 5" Crazy Edge Open Comport, 6" Crazy Edge Open Comport, 7" Crazy Edge Open Comport, 8" Crazy Edge Open Comport, 4" Covered Comport, 5" Covered Comport, 6" Covered Comport, 7" Covered Comport, 8" Covered Comport, One-half Gallon Pitcher, Goblet, Tumbler Style A, Tumbler Style B, Finger Bowl, Celery, 10" Salver, 4 1/2" Open Bowl, 5" Open Bowl, 6" Open Bowl, 7" Open Bowl, 8" Open Bowl, 4 1/2" Square Open Bowl, 5" Square Open Bowl, 6" Square Open Bowl, 7" Square Open Bowl, 8" Square Open Bowl, 4 1/2" Crazy Edge Open Bowl, 5" Crazy Edge Open Bowl, 6" Crazy Edge Open Bowl, 7" Crazy Edge Open Bowl, 8" Crazy Edge Open Bowl, 4 1/2" Covered Bowl, 5" Covered Bowl, 6" Covered Bowl, 7" Covered Bowl, 8" Covered Bowl, 10" Bowl Basket, and 12" Bowl Basket.

China, Glass & Lamps, January 10, 1894

The Columbia pattern is a plain pattern in clear glass that is usually engraved and always with the crimped edge. The goblet is crimped on the base. The items made in this pattern are as listed in the

Columbia Goblet, The pattern is the piecrust base, $85-110.

Columbia Water Pitcher, 1/2 Gallon, $125-145.

Paragon 1/2 Gal. Pitcher, clear, 9" high, $75-110.

Paragon Pattern, a.k.a. Kentucky

The second pattern to be placed on the market in 1894, by the firm, was the Paragon. *Dalzell, Gilmore & Leighton Co., of Findlay, Ohio, make a big display in their old quarters, room 156, where Mr. Lambie is on hand to receive visitors. One of their new tableware patterns is named the "Paragon", an appellation properly descriptive of its superior excellence, and the design is entirely new and distinct from any other that has appeared in the market. There is a full line of this and the set and jugs are especially noticeable for their elegance of shape and brilliancy. Another new pattern is the "Columbia", just placed on the market. This is the largest line they ever got out and has over 60 pieces. It is plain with a crimped edge and in the covered pieces the crimp is on the cover instead of the vessel itself thus making it easy to keep clean. The crimp is an elegant one, done by machinery altogether and is exact and uniform all around. They have the Columbia line in both plain and decorated. Of other patterns shown here, the "Genoese" and "49D" are still standard favorites with the trade and sell very freely. There are other lines there too and a big assortment of miscellaneous wares.*

Although there is no available record of the items made in this pattern, the quotation describes it as a

Columbia Cake Salver, $85-110.

Butler Brothers catalog, 1898

priced line, the "Amazon". They are making a special drive on jugs, having four new styles in half gallons, and offering altogether 19 different styles in tankard and squat shapes. They have a new patent molasses can, the top of which is put on without plaster, giving it advantages in the way of easy cleaning possessed by no other, and are having a big run on this class of goods. They are making something new in the way of molasses cans with extra large opening in the neck, and will make it a specialty, dropping the old style small opening. The Dalzell, Gilmore & Leighton Co. are now making a larger range of goods than ever before, and no longer have difficulty in making carload shipments from their own stock. They have lately put in gas producers and practically reconstructed their factory, putting in new lehrs and glory holes and increased their capacity 20 per cent.

Take notice the information about the production of Jugs (Pitchers). This undoubtedly is when the firm was making the many novelty type pitchers such as the Squirrel, Bicycle Girl, Bringing Home the Cows, Dog and Rabbit, and others. To be making this many in one season makes us realize that we will never know exactly what was made.

full line. With this we must assume that included would be the Covered Butter, Covered Sugar, Spoon, Cream, Celery, Half-Gallon Pitcher (Jug), Tumbler, Water Set, Berry Set, Bowls, Comports, and Goblet.

New Patterns for 1895

In the January 9, 1895, issue of *China, Glass and Lamps* we learn that:

> Dalzell, Gilmore & Leighton Co., of Findlay, Ohio, changed quarters this year, and now occupy room 23, where C. H. Lambie entertains callers in his customary suave manner. He has an exhibit this year of which he is especially proud, and one cannot blame him, for it is certainly attractive beyond the ordinary. In the forefront is the new "Alexis" pattern, consisting of three score and ten pieces of ware, each one of which is literally as pretty as a picture. The design is an original one, and it works out in the most brilliant ware possible to conceive, materials considered. The shallow flat dishes are unique in shape, closely following the best cut ware. Each cover is provided with a ball of crystal, so deftly put on that it is impossible to discover any mold marks. The jugs in this line are unequaled in purity and brilliancy. The mustards are wholly of glass, rendering them free from all possibility of corrosion. The individual sugars and creams are very pretty. The company are running now two fine lines, the "Alexis" and No. 57, the latter plain and engraved, and a medium

Alexis Pattern, a.k.a. Priscilla

The Alexis pattern is probably the most popular pattern made by the company. It was introduced in 1895. It has been reproduced in clear and color. The stars in the pattern are not as well formed in the reproductions and the original has been found in clear and ruby stain only. The ruby stain was applied at the Oriental Glass Company of Pittsburg, Pennsylvania.

Items manufactured in this pattern include the 4" Nappy, 4" Comport, 4 1/2" Flared Comport, 6" Flared Compote, 7" Flared Comport, 8" Flared Compote, 6" Square Comport, 7" Square Comport, 8" Square Comport, 6" Covered Comport, 7" Covered Comport, 8" Covered Comport, 4 1/2" Jelly Stand, 4 1/2" Covered Jelly, 6" Flared Bowl, 7" Flared Bowl, 8" Flared Bowl, 6" Square Bowl, 7" Square Bowl, 8" Square Bowl, 6" Covered Bowl, 7" Covered Bowl, 8" Covered Bowl, Bowl Basket, 10" Salver, Salver Basket, Salver Bowl, Covered Butter, Covered Sugar, Cream, Spoon, Half-gallon Tankard, Half-gallon Pitcher, Tumbler, Goblet, Wine, Celery, Shaker Salt, Shaker Pepper, Glass Lip Molasses Can, Molasses Can Plate, 6-oz. Vinegar Bottle, 5" Handled Nappy, Pickle Dish, Individual Cream, Individual Sugar and Cover, Toothpick, Mustard with Glass Lid, Lemonade, Custard Cup and Saucer, 6" Plate, Small Rose Jar, Medium Rose Jar, Large Rose Jar, Cracker Jar and Lid, Ice Jar, Finger Bowl, 9" Cabaret, 10" Cabaret, 12" Cabaret, 9" Banquet Stand, 10" Banquet Stand, 12" Banquet Stand, 5" Handled Flower

Basket, 9" Handled Flower Basket, and 10" Handled Flower Basket.

For reference, it should be noted that a Cabaret is a low heavy plate with turned up rim or a shallow bowl. Banquet stands are like the stacking of four open comports of graduating sizes with the smallest on the top.

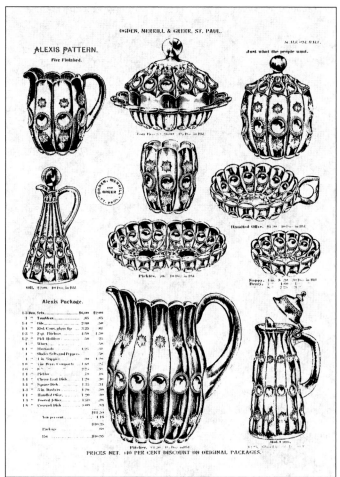

Ogden, Merrill & Greer catalog, 1895

Alexis Tankard Pitcher, 10 3/4" high, $125-175.
Alexis Bulbous Pitcher, 9 1/2" high, $135-195.
Best known as Priscilla, this pattern has always enjoyed popularity. It was made in clear glass and red flashed glass.

Alexis Tankard Water Pitcher, shown with a 7 1/2" vase made from the pitcher mold. A Spittoon made from the bulbous pitcher mold has been seen. These unusual pieces were not regular production items.

Alexis Rose Bowls, $45-65 ea.
Note the difference in height.

Side view of Alexis basket.

Alexis Five Inch Flower Basket, applied handle, $50-65.
Alexis Nine Inch Flower Basket, applied handle, $75-100.
Alexis Ten Inch Flower Basket, applied handle, $95-125.

Alexis Relish Dish, two part, 7 1/2" long, 5" wide, 1 1/2" high, $35-$45.

Alexis Salt and Pepper Shakers, 3" high, $75-100 pr.

Alexis Fruit Bowl, high standard, 8" high, 8" wide with pulled corners, $135-160.
Alexis Fruit Bowl, flat, 3" high, 8" wide, $35-45.

Alexis Covered Compote, 6", $45-65.
Alexis Covered Compote, 8", $45-65.
Alexis Covered Jelly Compote, 4 1/2", $85-110.
Alexis Covered Compote, 7", $45-65.

Alexis Large Rose Jar, 4 3/4" high, $50-75.
Alexis Small Rose Jar, 2 3/4" high, $45-65.
Alexis Medium Rose Jar, 3 3/4" high, $35-55.

Alexis Clover Leaf Dish, 7" wide, 1 1/2" high, $35-45.

Alexis Relish or Individual Table Set Tray:
Individual Covered Sugar, 4 1/4" high (with lid), 1 1/2" wide,
$50-65.
Covered Mustard, 3" high, 1 3/4" wide, $60-75.
Tray, 7 1/2" square, 1 1/2" high, $35-50.
Individual Cream, 3 3/4" high, $45-60.
Vinegar Cruet, 6 oz., 5-1/2" high, original ball stopper, $85-125.

Alexis Cake Salver, petticoat edge, 6 1/2" high, 9 3/4" wide,
$125-175.
Alexis Fruit Comport, petticoat edge, 8 1/4" high, 9 1/4" wide,
$135-175.

Alexis Syrup, 8 1/2" to top of the pewter lid, $90-150.
Alexis Under Plate, 5 1/2" wide, 1" high, $35-45.

Alexis Table Set:
Spoon Holder, 4 1/4" high, 3" wide, $45-65.
Celery, 5" high, 3 3/4" wide, $50-70.
Butter, 5-1/2" high with lid, 1 3/4" high without lid, $50-70.
Sugar bowl, 6" high with lid, 4" wide, $55-75.
Cream Pitcher, 5" high, 3" wide, $50-65.

Alexis Nappies and Finger Bowls, $25-40 ea.
Dalzell used the term nappy for the sauces illustrated. The ones
with the highest sides are Finger Bowls.

Alexis Lemonade Cup, $35-40.
Alexis Custard Cup, $35-40.

This photo shows the two different bases to the Cups. Note that while one has the star design, while the other has no design. In the bottom of the cup on the right is "VICORAL".

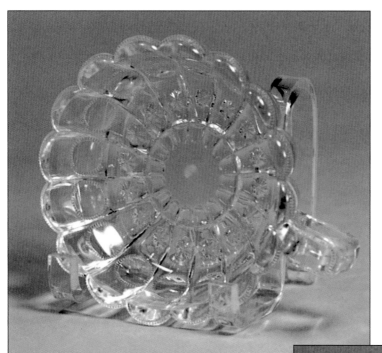

Alexis Five Inch Handled Nappy, $50-60.

Alexis Toothpick Holder, base illustrating advertising for wholesalers.

Alexis Toothpick Holder, $35-45.

Alexis Covered Bowl, 6" high with lid, 6" wide. True covered bowls have a more rounded shape than the open bowls, $95-135.

Alexia Goblet, clear, 5 7/8" high, 3 7/16" wide, $40-60.
Alexis Wine, 3 7/8" high, 2 9/16" wide, $35-45.

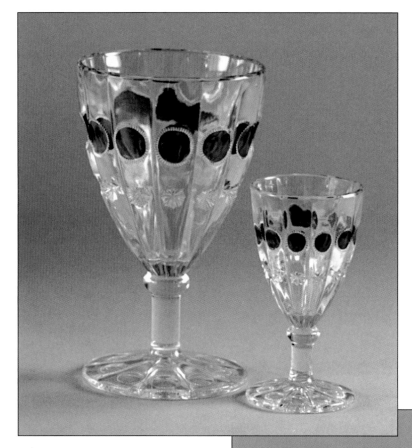

Alexis Goblet, Ruby
Stain, 5 7/8" high, 3 7/16"
wide, $120-140.
Alexis Wine, Ruby Stain,
3 7/8" high, 9/16" wide,
$120-140.

Alexis Tankard Pitcher, Ruby
Stain, $350-400.
Alexis Tumbler, Ruby Stain,
$125-165.

Alexis Spoon Holder, Ruby
Stain, 4 1/4" high, 3" wide,
$175-200.

57D Pattern, a.k.a. Corrigan

The Corrigan Pattern is another that must not have been a pattern to compete with the popularity of the Alexis because it is not plentiful for the collector.

This pattern has been found in clear, clear with engraving, and clear with a piecrust rim. Items made include the Butter and Cover, 6" Open Comport, 8" Open Comport, Sugar and Cover, Cream, Spoon, Celery, Half-gallon Tankard, Half-gallon Squat Pitcher, Tumbler, Wine, and a Berry Set. There are probably other pieces.

Corrigan Pitcher, clear, engraved, 11" high, 4 1/2" base, etched pitcher, $125-175.

G. Sommers and Co. catalog, 1895

Corrigan Salt and Pepper Shakers, clear, 3 1/4" high, 1 5/8" base, $75-100 pr.

Corrigan Syrup, clear, $135-175.

Corrigan, Spoon, clear, $65-90.
Corrigan, Butter, covered, clear, 5 1/2" high, 7 3/8" wide, $75-110.

Corrigan Covered Sugar, clear, 7" high, 4" wide, $45-60.
Corrigan Cream, clear, $45-60.

Corrigan Goblet, clear, 5 6/8" high, 3 1/8" wide, $45-60.
Corrigan Wine, clear, 3 7/8" high, 1 3/4" wide, $40-55.

Corrigan Pitchers, clear,
different shapes, $125-175
each.

Corrigan Covered Compote, clear, 9 1/2" high, 6" wide, $55-75.
Corrigan Covered Compote, clear, 12" high, 8" wide, $55-75.
Corrigan Covered Jelly Compote, clear, 7 1/4" high, 4 1/2" wide, $70-95.

Amazon Pattern, a.k.a. Double Fan

This is a pattern that gives credibility to the collector's name of Double Fan.

The Double Fan pattern is known in clear only. Items known are the Covered Butter, Covered Sugar, Cream, Spoon, Berry Set, Celery, Half-gallon Tankard, Half-gallon Squat Jug (pitcher), 4" Nappy, Relish, and Pickle Dish.

Ogden, Merrill & Greer catalog, 1895

Ogden, Merrill & Greer catalog, 1895

Amazon Water Pitcher, $95-135.

Patterns for 1897

This was a busy company, first making Lamps and Novelties their main products, and still adding new tableware lines each year as noted by a *China, Glass & Lamps* article of January 13, 1897, printed here in its entirety.

DALZELL, GILMORE & LEIGHTON: This well known firm have for many years made a specialty of all glass lamps, that it almost looks as though the manufacture of tableware had become a side line with them, and yet , just as if to keep in line, they get out a new pattern or two each year to amplify their assortment and impart variety to their lines. This year their new line consists of an imitation cut pattern called the Ivanhoe, the features of which are the covered bowls, cake stands, large berry bowls, handled oblong dishes, and especially their candy tray with a center pole or handle, making it convenient to handle which no candy tray has heretofore possessed. A plain, oval line has also been prepared for this season, suitable for engraving or etchings, and will prove out of the beaten path in tableware patterns. The company's exhibit is very strong in molasses jugs, the features of which are their large openings, pressed tops, and caps clinched on without the use of plaster or cement. Their line of pressed and blown lamps are also provided with clinched on collars, without plaster, and oil tight as well as explosive proof. In water jugs, plain and engraved, there are 21 different styles, as well as all sizes and styles of lamps, tumblers, goblets, and general tableware.

Pattern # 65D Ivanhoe

In the quoted article, the first mentioned pattern was the Ivanhoe. It has been found in clear only.

Items manufactured in the Ivanhoe pattern are 4" Berry Bowl, 7" Berry Bowl, Butter and Cover, Cake Salver, Center Handle Candy Dish, Carafe, Celery, 6"

Bowl, Cracker Jar, Cream, Cruet, Cup, Jelly Comport, 5" by 5" Dish, Handled Nappy, 8" Plate, 10" Plate, Relish, Individual Salt Dip, Master Salt, Salt Shaker, Pepper Shaker, Spoon, Sugar and Cover, Syrup, Toothpick Holder, Tumbler, Half-gallon Water Jug (Pitcher), Wine, 9" high Fruit Bowl, 9" high Cracker Jar and Cover, 12 1/2" high Comport and Cover, Water Bottle and Tumbler, and a 8" Footed Comport and Cover.

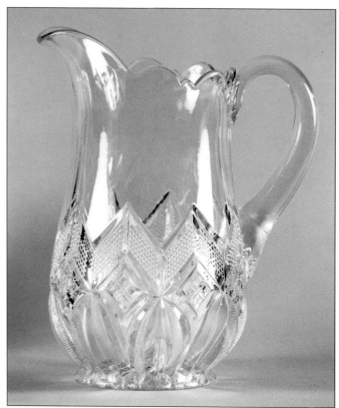

Ivanhoe Water Pitcher, clear, 10" high, 4 1/4" base diameter, bulbous shape, $95-150. Found in clear and ruby stain (Rare). This pattern has not been reproduced.

National Glass Company catalog, circa 1900

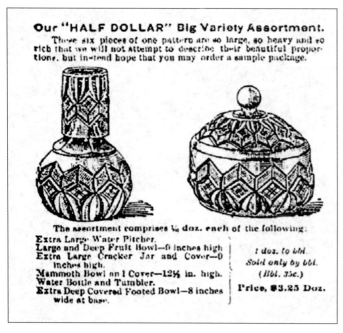

Butler Brothers catalog, 1898

Ivanhoe Salt Shaker, bulbous, clear, 3" high, $30-40.
Ivanhoe Salt Dip, clear, 1" high, 1 1/2" wide, $25-30.
Ivanhoe Salt Shaker, straight side, 3 1/8" high, $35-45.

Ivanhoe Handled Candy Dish, clear, 7 3/8" long, 6 1/4" wide, 1 1/4" high, (2 7/8" handle), $65-85.
Ivanhoe Nappy, clear, pear shape, 9 7/8" long w/handle, $35-50.

Ivanhoe clear syrup, $125-150.

Ivanhoe Cup, clear, 2 1/4" high, 2 7/8" wide, $25-35.
Ivanhoe Cruet, clear, 5 1/2" to top of spout, $95-125.
Ivanhoe Sauce, clear, 1 1/2" high, 4 1/2" wide, $15-20.

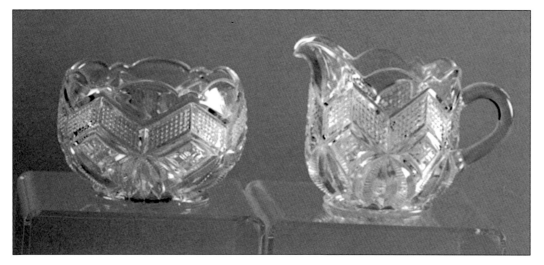

Ivanhoe Individual Open Sugar, clear, $35-40.
Ivanhoe Individual Cream, clear, $35-40.

Ivanhoe clear pitchers to illustrate the different shapes, $95-150 each.

Ivanhoe Compote, covered, clear, $65-80.

Ivanhoe Toothpick Holder, clear, 2 5/8" high x 2 1/8" diameter, $125-140.

Pattern #74D
Beaded Medallion

The Beaded Medallion pattern might have been called plain by the writer of the article in *China, Glass and Lamps*, and it probably was when compared to the Ivanhoe pattern. In actuality, it was beautiful. It was available in clear, clear with engraving, emerald green, and emerald green with engraving. There were many decorations made that we have no knowledge of and for that reason there may be many pieces of amber or ruby stain. The pattern was made for all kinds of decoration.

Known items in the Beaded Medallion include a 7" Berry Bowl, 8 1/2" Bowl, 11" Banquet Stand, Butter and Cover, 9" Cake Stand, Celery, 6" Comport and Cover, Cream, Cruet, Plate, Spoon, Sugar and Cover, Syrup, Half-gallon Jug (Pitcher), Tumbler, and Berry Set.

74 D Sugar and Cover.

National Glass Co. catalog, circa 1900

Bowl and Cover.

National Glass Co. catalog, circa 1900

Beaded Medallion Compote, open, emerald green, $95-135.

Beaded Medallion Spoon Holder, clear, $35.

Beaded Medallion Fruit Comport, emerald green, $95-135.

Beaded Medallion Tumbler, emerald green, $70-110 ea.

Pattern 75D Amberette

The original advertisement in *China, Glass & Lamps* had the name as Amberette and noted that it was known as 75D in clear. We must add that it also can be called 75D Emerald Green since a Salt Shaker in this color has been found. The Amberette is clear with amber stain and frosted. This pattern was first announced as a new pattern for 1898 in *China, Glass & Lamps* on December 22, 1897.

Dalzell, Gilmore & Leighton Co., of Findlay, Ohio, have a very handsome square line to place on the market January 1. They will have it decorated in an entirely different manner from any hitherto offered. They will also have a short line, footed, that is exceptionally bright, and a cheaper unfinished. They are making a tea, water berry set of colored glass, comprising two colors, with various decorations different from anything that have ever been placed on the market. They will have more new goods to show this time than in any former season, and will occupy their old room, No. 70, at the Monongahela House.

This announcement was followed by an article of January 5, 1898, which stated that: *C. H. Lambie, another of the old timers, looks after the interests of Dalzell, Gilmore & Leighton Co., Findlay, Ohio, in room 70. He has a brand new line called Amberetta on his tables, which is probably the most original and unique in de-sign of any shown this season. The shapes are generally square, though there are some rectangular and oval pieces, and there are narrow bands of neat small figuring crossing one another at the bottom, coming up the sides and going horizontally around each of the articles. They have this in plain crystal and also with the figured part in amber, and the effect is very striking and brilliant. They have it in transparent glass as well as satin finish and the latter presents a most pleasing appearance. They have a lot of jugs and several low priced lines too, but the Amberetta is their leader for this season, and those who see it will agree with us in saying that it is an attractive novelty in table glass.*

This pattern is rated as desirable a pattern as the famous Onyx. Over the years writers have credited it to other companies, but catalogs and trade journals bear out the fact that it was only the product of Dalzell, Gilmore and Leighton. The items available are a 7" Bowl, 9" Bowl, 8" Berry, 10" Bouquet Holder, Butter and Cover, 10" Celery Tray, Claret, 8 1/2" Confection, Condiment Set, Cream, Cruet, Cup, Goblet, Bulbous Salt, Bulbous Pepper, Straight Salt, Straight Pepper, Spoon, Sugar and Cover, Toothpick, Tumbler, 57 oz. Square Jug, 32 oz. Round Jug, Wine, Handled Nappy, 9" Pickle, 9" Plate, 9" Oval Dish, 8" Salad Dish, Syrup, 8" Vase (Snyder), 7" Vase, and 8" Vase.

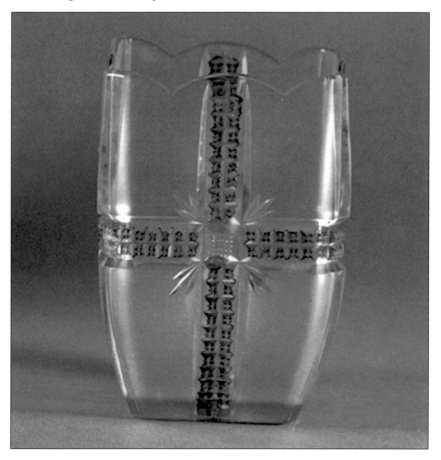

75D, Amberette Celery Vase, 5 7/8" high, 4" wide, $375-400.
It is the most difficult shape to find in this pattern.

DALZELL, GILMORE & LEIGHTON COMPANY,
FINDLAY, OHIO.

Something entirely new and handsome, the panels are satin finished, the figured bands are stained old gold, while the deep mitres on either side are bright crystal, giving the most striking and beautiful effect of anything ever placed on the market. The line consists of 40 pieces of the most beautiful articles for table use.

AMBERETTE WARE.

Amberette Ware in crystal is known as 75 D, it is an exceptionally bright pattern, the shapes are striking and orginal.

Samples may be seen until February 5th at Room 70 Mononghela House, Pittsburgh, Pa.
Ask your jobber for cuts and prices.

China, Glass & Lamps, January 20, 1898

Butler Brothers catalog, 1900

75D, Amberette Syrup with pewter lid, 8" to top of lid, 3 1/2" wide, $450-500.

75D, Amberette Toothpick Holder, 1 1/2" high, 2 3/8" wide, $400-450.
75D, Toothpick Holder, clear, 1 1/2" high, 2 3/8" wide, $125-150.

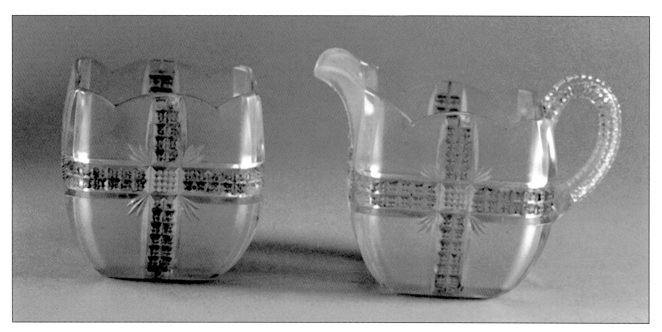

75D, Amberette Spoon, 3 3/8" high, 3 1/2" wide, $250-275.
75D, Amberette Cream, 3 5/8" high, 4" wide, $275-300.

75D, Amberette Covered Sugar, 6" high, 4 1/2" wide, $275-325.

75D, Amberette Wine, 3 3/4" high, 1 7/8" wide, $600-700.
75D, Wine, clear, 3 3/4" high, 1 7/8" wide, $125-150.
75D, Amberette Wine, the Amberette is a lighter color, $600-700.

75D, Amberette Covered Butter, 6" high, 6 7/8" square, $275-325.

122

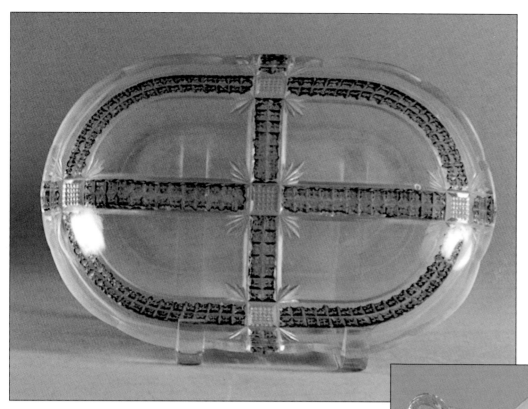

75D, Amberette Bowl, oval, 2 3/4" high, 9" x 6 1/4" oval, $175-225.

75D, Amberette Pitcher, round, 10" high, 4 1/2" base, $350+.
75D, Amberette Pitcher, square, 8 3/4" high, 4 5/8" square, $350+.

75D, Amberette Goblet, 6 1/8" high, 3 1/4" wide, $300+.
75D, Amberette Wine, $600-700.
75D, Amberette Champagne, 5 1/2" tall, 3" wide. This is the most sought after of all the stemmed Amberette and 75D clear, $700-850.

75D, Vase, clear with frosted panels, 8 1/2" high, 3 3/8" wide, $35-45.
75D, Vase, Amberette, 8 1/2" high, 3 3/8" wide, $85-110.
75D, Vase, clear, 8 1/2" high, 3 3/8" wide, $35-40.

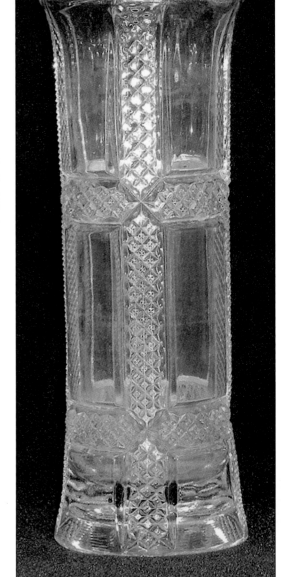

75D, Vase, clear, 8" high, 3" wide, the Snyder vase with no decoration, $1,000. This is more difficult to find than the decorated.

75D, Amberette Vase, 8" high, 3" wide, $1,800+.
This is the most difficult vase to find. It is also found in clear.
This was named the Snyder Vase by Findlay researcher Don Smith.

75D, Amberette
Vase, 7", $65-80.
75D, Amberette
Vase, 8", $65-80.

75D, Canoe Shape Relish, clear, 9" x 3 3/8", 1 3/8" high, $65-80.
75D, Amberette Canoe Shape Relish, 9" x 3 3/8", 1 3/8" high,
$110-135.

75D, Vase, clear, 7", $35-40.
75D, Vase, clear, 8", $35-40.

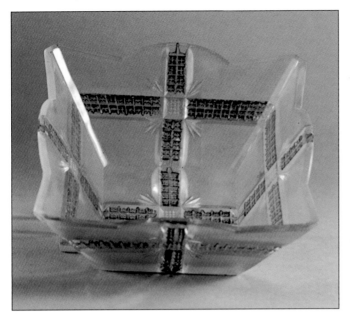
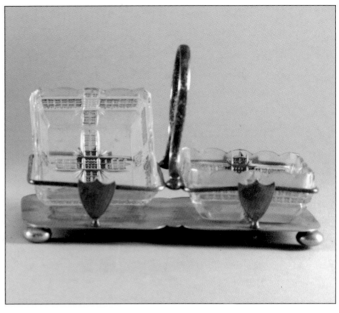

75D, Amberette Bowl, slanted sides, 3 1/4" x 7 1/4", $90-110.

75D, Amberette Condiment Set of two 2 3/4" high by 4" square trays in a silver-plated holder, $2,000+.

75D, Amberette Salt and Pepper, bulbous, 2 7/8" high, 1 7/8" sq., $250-300.
75D, Clear, Salt and Pepper, tall, 3 3/4" high, 1 3/8" wide, $185-245.

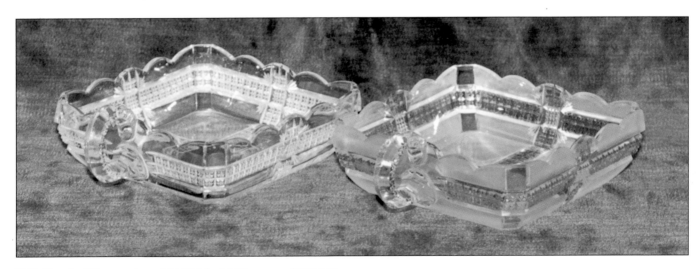

75D, Handled Nappy, clear, 1 3/4" high, 5 1/4" square, $125-145.
75D, Amberette Handled Nappy, 1 3/4" high, 5 1/4" square, $145-170.

75D, Amberette Condiment Set, $2,000+.
This set includes the 5 1/2" high Cruet, 7/8" x 5 3/4" Tray, 2 3/4" high Toothpick Holder, and the Tall Salt and Pepper Shakers.

75D Condiment Set, clear, $1,200+.
This set includes the 5 1/2" Cruet, 7/8" x 5 3/4" Tray, 2 3/4" Toothpick Holder, and the Bulbous Salt and Pepper Shakers.

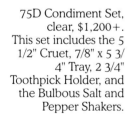

75D, Amberette Celery Tray, 10", $160-195.
75D, Celery Tray, 10", $145-165.

75D, Emerald Green Salt Shaker, $1,200+.
This is the only piece in this color reported at this time. It is
extremely rare. The Beaded Medallion was being produced in the same time period in the same emerald green
so there were probably other pieces made.

Pattern #77D, a.k.a. Retort

The Retort pattern is a pattern that is not easily found but makes a beautiful collection. It is known in clear only. This was a pattern of 1899.

Items found in the Retort pattern are a Berry Set, 7" Square Bowl, Butter and Cover, Celery, Cream Jug, 10" Flared Fruit Dish, Jelly Comport, Handled Nappy, 9" Pickle, Master Salt, Individual Salt Dip, Spoon, Sugar and Cover, Square Tray, Toothpick, and 42 oz. Water Jug.

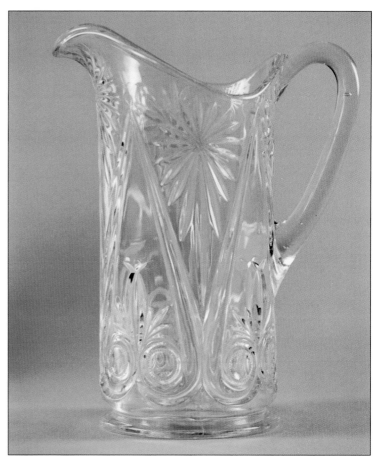

Retort 1/2 Gal. Jug, 9 1/2" high with 4 1/2" base, $125-175.
The glass in this pattern is usually very clear and brilliant. Made only in clear glass.

National Glass Company catalog, circa 1900

6 77 D Water Jug, 42 oz.

National Glass Company catalog, circa 1900

Retort Butter, clear, 5 1/2" to top of knob on lid, 5 1/4" wide at base of lid, 8" widest spot on base, $150-200.

Retort Syrup, clear, 8" high to top of nickel-plated lid, $125-175.

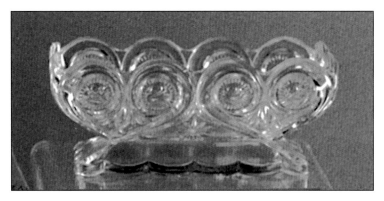

Retort Master Salt, clear, 1 1/2" high, 4" long, 2 7/8" wide, $35-50.

Retort Bowl, round, clear, 8 1/2", $40-55.
Retort Banana Dish, clear, $45-60.

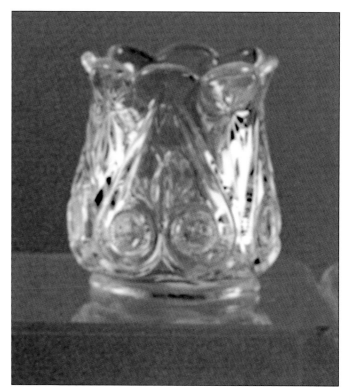

Retort Toothpick Holder, clear, 2 7/8" high, $60-85.

Retort Jelly Compote, clear, $35-45.

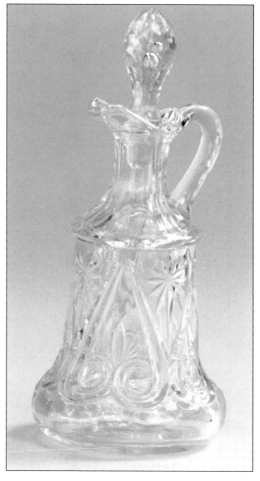

Retort Cruet, clear, $135-160.

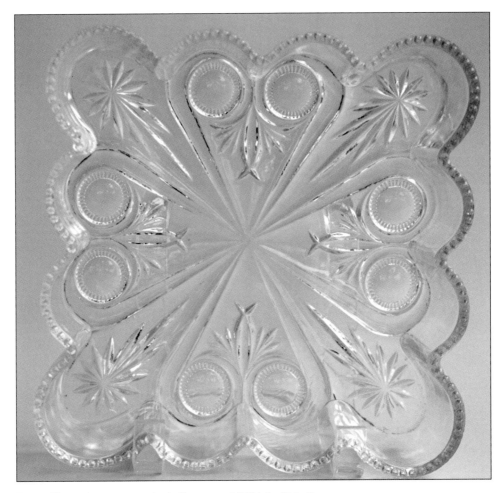

Retort Plate, clear, square, 6 7/16" square, 7/8" high, $35-40.

Retort Salt Shaker,
clear, $65-75.

Pattern # 79D,
a.k.a. Serrated Teardrop

This pattern can be found in clear, white opaque, and emerald green. Both the clear and emerald green are found with engraving. This pattern was introduced in 1900.

Serrated Teardrop was made in many items, including a Berry Set, 8" Oval Bowl, 9 1/2" Bread Tray, Butter and Cover, 8 1/2" Cake Tray, Celery, Cream, Cruet, Jelly Comport and Cover, 9" Oblong Pickle, Squat 48 oz. Water Jug, Tankard Jug, Pepper Shaker, Salt Shaker, Spoon, Sugar and Cover, Syrup, 5 3/4" High Footed Tray, Tumbler, and Toothpick.

National Glass Company catalog, circa 1900

"GOLD ENGRAVED" Misc. Asst. (No. C342.) *367

The heavy pure gold applied on the deeply engraved floral spray gives the inlaid effect so much sought in glass.

—The assortment comprises the following:

1/6	Doz.	4-Piece Table Sets	$6 30	$1 05
1/4	"	Tankard Water Pitchers	2 40	60
1 1/2	"	Large Table Tumblers	70	1 05
1/6	"	High Celéry Dishes	1 80	30
1/4	"	Oil or Vinegar Cruets	1 80	45
1/6	"	Syrup Cans—Fine top	2 00	34
1	"	Salts and Peppers—Assorted	43	43
1/4	"	8-inch Berry Nappies	1 60	40
1 1/2	"	4 " Sauce or Berry Nappies	42	63
1/3	"	Flower Vases—8 inches	80	27
1/3	"	8½-inch Oval Cake Trays	1 00	33
1/6	"	9½ " Bread Trays	1 20	20
1/6	"	5¾ " High Footed Fancy Trays or Jellies	1 20	20

(All in bbl., wt. 98 lbs. Bbl. 25c.) **Total—$6.25**

Butler Brothers catalog, 1901

Serrated Teardrop Water Pitcher, clear, 10 1/4" high, $75-95.
This pattern can be found in clear, green, and opaque white. Some pieces were engraved with berries and leaves painted gold. Opaque pieces were always plain.

Serrated Teardrop
Toothpick Holder,
clear, 2 3/8" high and
2 1/4" wide, $65-85.

Serrated Teardrop Salt and Pepper Shakers, emerald green, 3 1/4" high, $50-75 pr.
Serrated Teardrop Salt Shaker, opaque white, 3 1/4" high, $35-45.

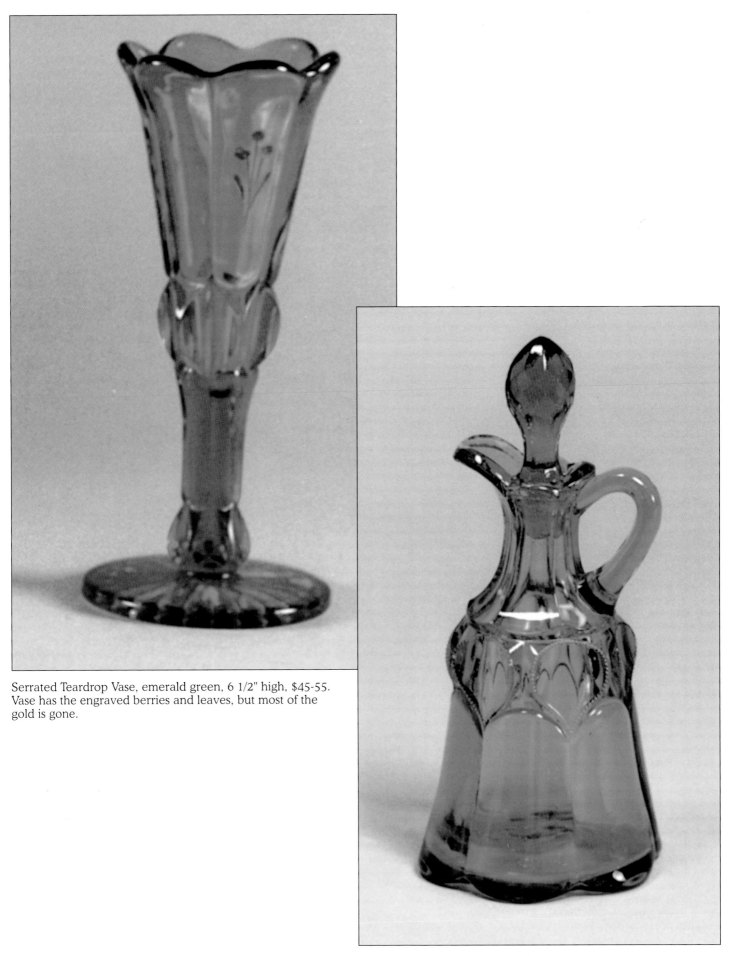

Serrated Teardrop Vase, emerald green, 6 1/2" high, $45-55.
Vase has the engraved berries and leaves, but most of the
gold is gone.

Serrated Teardrop Cruet, emerald green, $125-195.

Serrated Teardrop Tumbler, clear, $45-65.
Serrated Teardrop Jelly Compote, clear, $55-65.
Serrated Teardrop Cruet, clear, $110-145.

Serrated Teardrop Water Set, green, $450-525.

Serrated Teardrop Spoon Holder, clear, engraved, $40-50.

Serrated Teardrop 1/2
Gal. Pitcher, clear,
$85-125.

Serrated Teardrop
Butter, covered,
$60-85.

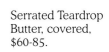

Pattern # 81 D Daphne, a.k.a. Wellsburg

Wellsburg was a pattern of 1901 and was made in clear and clear decorated with ruby stain and clear with frosted panels.

Items made are an 11" Banquet Stand, 7" Drop Corner Berry, 8" Drop Corner Bowl, 8" Massive Bowl, 10" Cupped Berry, Butter and Cover, 12 1/2" Cabaret Cake Salver, Celery, 7" Covered Comport, Cream, Cruet, 9" Oval Dish, 8" Fruit Bowl, Handled Olive, Jelly Comport and Cover, Mug, 8 1/2" Handled Pickle, Punch Bowl, Punch Cup, 8" Salad Bowl, Spoon, Sugar and Cover, Syrup, Toothpick, Tumbler, and a 54 oz. Water Jug.

Daphne Pitcher, 11 1/2" to top of spout, 4 1/2" base, $125-$150.
Several different colors were used in decorating this pattern (red, yellow, gold,).
It is most beautiful when frosted.

Daphne Condiment Set:
Toothpick Holder, frosted, 2 3/8"
high, 2" wide, $95-125.
Salt and Pepper Shakers, frosted,
3" high, $85-125 pr.
Cruet, frosted, 6 3/4" to top of
stopper, $100-125.
Tray, frosted, 6 1/4" square, 1/4"
deep, $35-45.

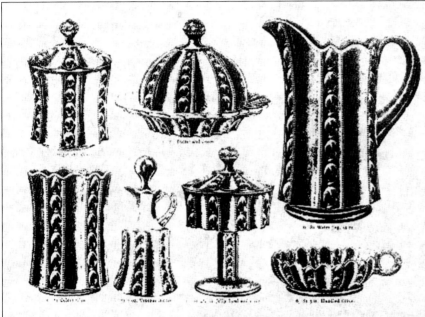

National Glass Company catalog,
circa 1900

Daphne Syrup, frosted panels,
6 1/4" to top of pewter lid,
$125-175.
Daphne Syrup, clear, 6 1/4" to
top of pewter lid, $95-135.

Daphne Spoon Holder, gold decorated, 3 3/4" high, 3 1/2" wide, $65-80.
Daphne Open Sugar, gold decorated, 4" high, 4" wide, $50-65.
Daphne Butter, gold decorated, 5" high, 8" wide, $85-110.
Daphne Cream Pitcher, 4 1/2" high, 2 5/8" base, $50-75.

Daphne Spoon Holder, yellow stain decoration on beads, 4 1/2" high, $75-110.

Daphne Mug, 2 7/8" high, 2 1/2" wide, $45-55.
Daphne Custard Cup, 2 3/4" high, 2 3/4" wide, $35-45.

Daphne Jelly Compote, covered, 7" high, 4 1/2" wide, $75-90.

Daphne Tall Tumbler, 5"
high, 3 1/4" wide, $50-65.
Daphne Tumbler, frosted, 4"
high, 2 3/4" wide, $55-65.

Daphne Relish, kidney-
shaped, 8 3/4" wide at front,
5" wide at handle, 1 3/8"
high, $35-45.

Daphne Toothpick Holder, gold
decorated beads, 2 3/8" high, 2" wide,
$70-80.
Daphne Toothpick Holder, ruby stain, 2
3/8" high, 2" wide, $300-350.
Daphne Toothpick Holder, clear, 2 3/
8" high, 2" wide, $65.
Daphne Toothpick Holder, gold
panels, 2 3/8" high, 2" wide, $70-80.

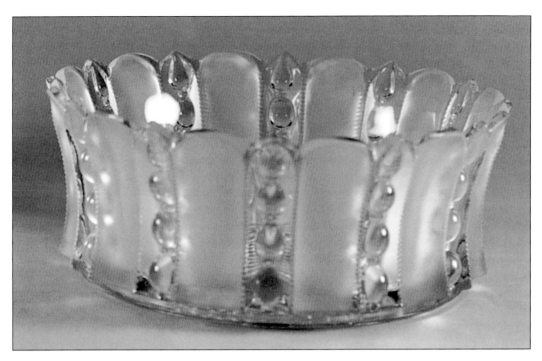

Daphne Oval Bowl, 2 3/4" high, 9" long, 6" wide, $45-55.

Daphne Cracker Jar, frosted panels, 8" high to top of
knob on lid, 5 1/8" wide, $135-165.

Pattern 83D,
a.k.a. Reeding Band

Reeding Band is a shorter line and was produced in the year of closing. This is a pattern of unique shape of some items. While the Water Bottle is bulbous, as most are, it has the bands, but also a ribbed pattern on the bulbous part. This is the only piece of this pattern with the ribs. The salt and pepper have different shapes. The salt has straight sides while the pepper has slanted sides.

Items known in Reeding Bands are the Berry Set, Butter and Cover, Cream Jug, Spoon, Sugar and Cover, Pepper, Salt, 6 oz. Syrup Jug, Tumbler, 1/2 Gallon Water Jug, and a 34 oz. Water Bottle.

OUR "NEWEST" HIGH TANKARD JUG.

A jug of quarter quality for a bargain price.

C458—With large handle and wide base. Full finished. Regular so-called half gallon. Just the jug to run at say 15c on "Star Day." (*2 dozen in bbl., wt. 103 lbs. Barrel 35c.*) Per dozen, **$1.25**

Butler Brothers catalog, 1902

National Glass Company catalog, circa 1900

Reeding Band Tankard Water Pitcher, clear, $ 125-150.

146

Pattern # 85D Delos

This was the last production pattern at the Dalzell, Gilmore & Leighton Glass Works. This is a very plain pattern and lent itself very well to engraving and staining. It has been found in clear, ruby stain, and both with engraving.

Items found in Delos are Square Berry Set, Round Berry Set, Butter and Cover, Cake Salver, Celery, 6" Open Comport, 7" Open Comport, 8" Open Comport, 4 1/2" Covered Comport, 6" Covered Comport, 7" Covered Comport, 8" Covered Comport, 11" Fruit Bowl, 4 1/2" Jelly Comport, 72 oz. Pitcher, 5" Rose Bowl, Sugar and Cover, Toothpick, Tumbler, and Custard Cup.

Butler Brothers catalog, 1902

Butler Brothers catalog, 1902

Delos Toothpick Holder, 2 3/8" high, 2 1/4" wide, $60-75.

Delos Covered Compotes, high standard, $85-135 ea.

147

Pattern Hexagonal Bull's Eye

This has been an elusive pattern to determine when it was made and what the pattern number might be. It appears that it should be in the 70s numbering but we cannot be certain. For this reason, we are not going to make guesses or speculate in any manner, but simply list the information that is available. This is one pattern for which we could not locate an illustration, but we have photos in the photo section.

Items are in clear and some amber stain. Items found are a Berry Set, Butter and Cover, Celery, 10" Comport and Cover, Cracker Jar and Cover, Cream, Goblet, Half Gal. Jug (Pitcher), Tumbler, Spoon, Sugar and Cover, and a Cake Salver.

Hexagonal Bullseye Fruit Bowl, $85-125.

Hexagonal Bullseye Condiment Tray, $85-110.

Miscellaneous Items

This company also made many patterns with a small number of items such as goblet only and pitcher only. We will attempt to list them all, but probably will not be successful as many items were manufactured and not attributed, especially novelty type items.

In Squat Pitchers there is the Squirrel, Three Birds, Branched Tree, and Racing Deer and Doe.

In the Tankard Pitchers are Bicycle Girl, Bringing Home the Cows, Dog and Rabbit, and Fox and Crow.

A Candy Dish is in the Edna Pattern and exists in Blue, Vaseline, and Clear.

Bow and Jewel Tumbler, $45-65.

Sunburst and Teepee Syrup, $145-170.

Sunburst and Teepee Goblet, $65-85.

Concave Lens Cup, $35-50.

Diamond and Bow Pitcher, $65-85.

Plume and Fan Butter Dish, clear, 4 1/2" high, base 6 1/4" wide, lid 4 1/16" wide, $50-65.
Plume and Fan Spoon Holder, clear, 4 5/8" high, 3 1/4" wide at top, $40-55.
Plume and Fan was one of the late patterns produced at the Findlay factory. The original number or name is not known. This is a very difficult pattern to find.

Plume and Fan 1/2 Gal. Water Pitcher, clear, 8 1/4" high, 4 1/2" base, $75-90.

No. 18D, a.k.a. Knurled Band Goblet, blue, $48-60.

No. 18D, a.k.a. Knurled Band Goblet, clear, $28-40.

Thrush Salt and Pepper Shakers, white opaque, 2 1/4" high, $100-150 pr.
Only the salt and pepper shakers were made in this pattern.

Thrush salt shaker showing some of the excess glass on the top,
just as it was when it came from the mold. It was never finished.

No. 18D mold without the band, amber
stain in floral engraving, $65-80.

"D" Rhea – Protruding Panels, Vertical, Salt and Pepper Shakers, white opaque, 2 1/4" high, $85-110 pr.
NOTES: This pattern was named by Don Smith in his book *Findlay Pattern Glass*. He named it for the lady who got him interested in knowing more about the glass that was made in Findlay, Ohio, in 1800s.

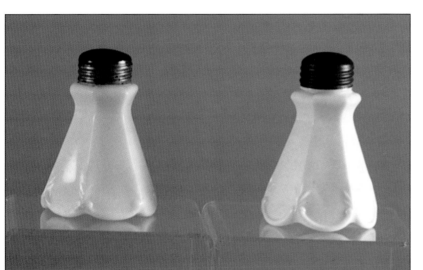

Hexagon Pyramid Salt and Pepper Shakers, white opaque, 3" high, $75-100 pr.

Robbins Salt and Pepper Shakers, white opaque, 2 5/8", $50-75 pr.
Found only in white opaque. This is another pattern named by Don Smith in his book. Robbins was named for Mrs. "Bobbie" Robbins who was an early antique dealer in Findlay, Ohio. She helped Mr. Smith locate some of the pieces shown in his book and shared her knowledge with him.

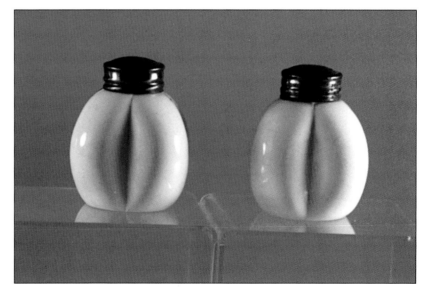

Square Twist Salt and Pepper Shakers, white opaque, 3 1/2" high, $80-110 pr.
Square Twist is found only in white opaque.

Square Twist Salt Shaker showing the original factory hand-painted design.

Little Orphan (NBA) Salt Shaker, white opaque, 3" high, $65-85.
This is a recently found shaker.

Pretty Panels (NBA) Salt and Pepper Shakers, white opaque, 3"
high, $75-95 pr.
Previously not named.

Staple Band Syrup, clear, 5" to the top of the shoulder where the
top rests, $85-125.
Staple Band Syrup, white opaque, 5" to the top of the shoulder
where the top rests, $85-125.
Clear syrup has a tin top. Opaque syrup has a nickel-plated lid.
This is the same design as used on the #79 Serrated Teardrop
lamp font.

Beaded Drape Syrup, white opaque, 7 3/4" high (to top of lid),
$85-125.
Beaded Drape Salt and Pepper Shakers, white opaque, 3 1/4"
high, $75-90 pr.

Edna Sugar Bowl,
Vaseline, $500+.

Edna Sugar Bowl, blue, $500+.
The sugar bowl is the only shape that has been found—a very elusive pattern to find.

Bulging Bars Toothpick Holder, $90.

Bulging Bars Wine Glass,
$60-70.

Squirrel and Nut Pitcher, clear, 8 3/4" high to top of spout, 4 1/4" base, $175-225.
5D shaped pitcher.

Smith Pitcher, clear, 9 1/2" high, 4 1/2" base, $95-125.
The only time that Don Smith allowed himself any vanity was in naming this beautiful water pitcher after himself. Only found in clear glass. There is a tumbler to match.

Heron Pitcher, clear, 8 3/4" high, 4 1/4" base, $250-300.
5D shape pitcher.

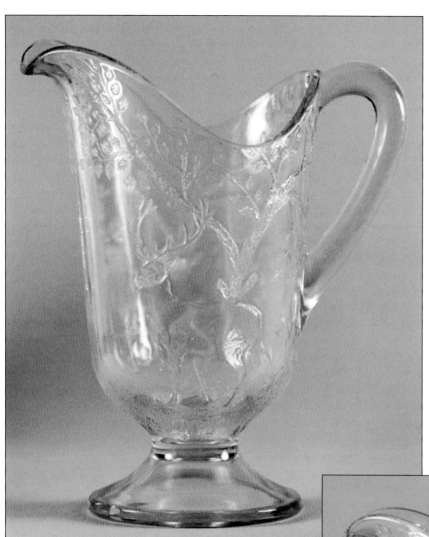

Deer Alert Pitcher, clear, 8 3/4" high, 4 1/4" base,
$150-225.

Racing Deer Pitcher, clear, 8 3/4"
high, 4 1/2" base, $150-225.
5D shape pitcher found in clear
glass only.

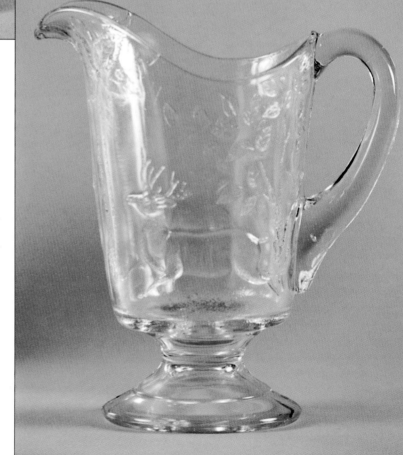

Branched Tree Pitcher, clear, 8 1/2" high to top of spout, 4 1/2" base, $95-125.
Branched Tree was made only in a water pitcher. It is the same shape as the animal series. Found in clear only.

Deer and Oak Tree, clear, 8 1/2" high, 4 1/2" base pitcher, $125-200.
Another pitcher of the animal series, it is only found in clear glass.

Three Birds Pitcher, clear, 9" high, $200-350.

Left:
Bicycle Girl Pitcher, clear, 10 3/4" high, $1,200-1,600. This is one of the most sought after of all the Findlay water pitchers. It has been found in green, and chocolate glass. The mold was taken to Indiana Goblet and Tumbler Co. where it was made in chocolate glass. The green pitchers could have been produced at both factories.

This is the reverse side of the Three Birds Pitcher.

Bring Home the Cows Pitcher, clear, 10 1/2" high, $1,200-1,500. The companion pitcher to the Bicycle Girl is only seen in clear. It was made in other colors by the National Glass Company.

Pitcher, Swirl, clear, $125-140. Difficult pitcher to find.

Pitcher, plain, clear, 19 1/2" high,
$125-140.
Same shape as Bring Home the
Cows pitcher.

Flutes and Diamonds, NBA, Pitcher, clear, $150+.
Same basic shape as the Bring Home the Cows. Design is on the
outside of the pitcher.

Ebony Flute, NBA, Pitcher, black, $350+.
There is a fluted pattern on the interior of this piece. Made in
clear also.

Pitcher, clear, 10 3/4" high,
$125+.
Pitcher, clear, 7 3/4" high, 3
1/2" base, $125+.
The large pitcher is of the
same shape and size as the
Girl on the Bicycle pitcher
and Ebony Flute.

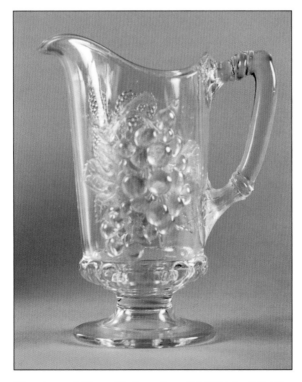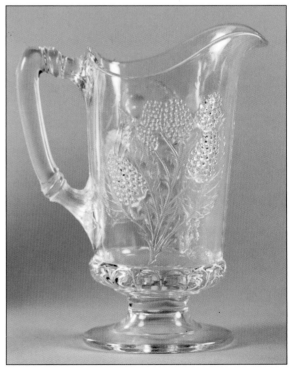

Cherries and Grape Pitcher, clear, 8 1/4" high, $75-95.
NOTES: Made of clear glass and done with several different fruits.

Squirrel Pitcher, $175-225.

Thread and Lens Pitcher, clear, $75-95.

232-64—Hand engraved $3 50
232—Plain, extra large...... .... 2 50

Ogden, Merrill & Greer catalog, 1895

Beaded Fine Cut Spoon Holder, $35-50.
Beaded Fine Cut Cream Pitcher, $35-50.

Bird. 11 ½-gallon Pitcher

Ogden, Merrill & Greer catalog

Squirrel Half-gallon Pitcher

Ogden, Merrill & Greer catalog

Salt and pepper shakers were made in Rhea-D, Robbins, Square Twist, and Hexagonal Pyramid. These are mostly in Opal glass and are sometimes fitted with a screw on burner to make a night-light. These patterns were also made in Syrup Pitchers.

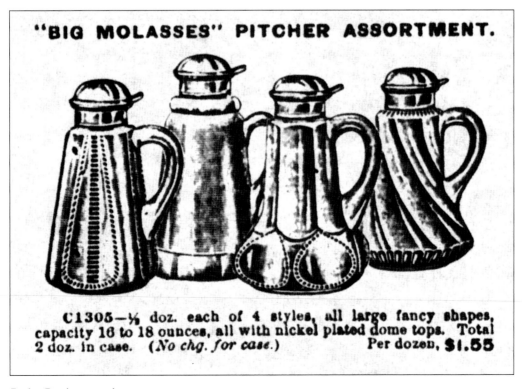

"BIG MOLASSES" PITCHER ASSORTMENT.

C1305—⅙ doz. each of 4 styles, all large fancy shapes, capacity 16 to 18 ounces, all with nickel plated dome tops. Total 2 doz. in case. (*No chg. for case.*)   Per dozen, **$1.55**

Butler Brothers catalog

Patterns for Cambridge.

When the last months of the Dalzell, Gilmore & Leighton Works were coming to an end, there was no reason to produce new lines of tableware. The mold makers at the firm were busy, however, making molds for two new patterns for the new Cambridge factory. Although a few test pieces were probably made, there was no production of these two patterns. One pattern is known as Teardrop and Cracked Ice. This was the Cambridge No. 2501 ware. The second pattern was the Deep File and was the Cambridge No. 2502 pattern.

Teardrop and Cracked Ice Salt and Pepper Shakers, clear, 3" high, 1 1/4" base, $65-85.

Teardrop and Cracked Ice Cruet, the stopper is not original. 6" high to top of spout, 2 1/4" wide at base, $95-125.
The molds for this pattern were transferred to the National Glass Co. factory at Cambridge, Ohio, and became their No. 2501 pattern. It has been found only in clear.

Teardrop and Cracked Ice Celery, clear, 6" high, 3 7/8" wide at top, $55-75.
Teardrop and Cracked Ice Vase, clear, 8 1/2" high, 3 1/2" wide at top, $50-70.
Teardrop and Cracked Ice Toothpick Holder, clear, 2 3/4" high, 2 1/4" wide at top, $95-135.
Teardrop and Cracked Ice Mug, clear, 3 1/2" high, 2 3/4" wide at top, $35-50.

Deep File Jelly Compote, clear, 5" high, 4 1/2" wide at top, $40-60. The molds for this pattern were moved to the Cambridge Glass Company and became their No. 2502.

Teardrop and Cracked Ice Vase, clear, 6 1/2" high, $45-75.
Teardrop and Cracked Ice Vase, clear, 8 1/2" high, $50-80.

Deep File Salt and Pepper Shakers, clear, 3 3/4" high, 1 1/16" wide at base, $50-80 pr.

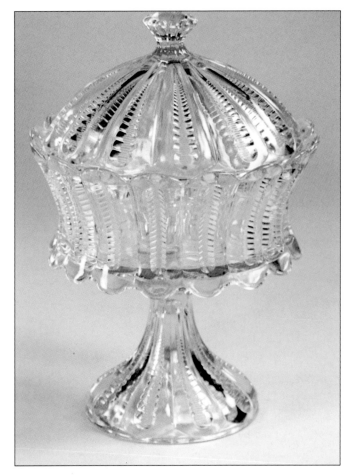

Deep File Covered Compote, clear, 11" to top of knob on lid, 8 1/4" wide, $125-155.

Deep File Salt Cellar, clear, 1 1/4" high, 1 3/4" wide, $30-45.
Deep File Toothpick Holder, clear, 2 3/4" high, 2" wide at top, $50-75.

Deep File Salt and Pepper Shakers, clear, 3 1/2" high, 1 1/16" wide, $50-80.

Lamps

From the beginning, The Dalzell, Gilmore & Leighton Company found that making and selling of lamps was a profitable business. Before the move to Findlay, it was noted in *Pottery and Glassware Reporter* in 1885, that they had a good seller in their Lighthouse Lamp. It was produced in A, B, C, and D sizes.

William A. B. Dalzell was issued a patent on February 26, 1898, for a *Force Fit Collar*. This collar resembles the Riverside clinch on collar in appearance only. The patent number for this collar is 658,171. It was assigned to the Dalzell, Gilmore & Leighton Glass Company.

Philip Ebeling was issued a patent for a machine that applied these collars to lamps on November 12, 1899. It was patent number 642,307 and was also assigned to the firm.

Philip Ebeling was issued a patent for a machine to be used for the manufacture of lamps in one piece. Heretofore, lamps were made by joining the font and base after they had been made separately. This was one of the reasons that the National Glass Company wanted the Dalzell, Gilmore & Leighton Company, so that they could have this machinery to use at their Ohio Flint and McKee glass works. This was such a radical change in the production of lamps that the firm's management and the President of the Flint Glass Workers Union had to negotiate a set of wages for the members working on a lamp machine.

On June 1, 1900, it was announced that the Marvin Machine Company was to build an additional twelve lamp machines.

The best information is either from factory catalogs or the trade journals of the day. With this in mind, let us give you a few of the writings.

From the *Crockery and Glass Journal* of November 1, 1888: *Dalzell, Gilmore & Leighton Co. are firing their third furnace and getting ready to make a steady run on fine holiday goods. They are now turning out some elegant designs in ruby and opalescent shades and other goods in rich colors.*

The 1889 production of lamps was highlighted by the introduction of the Onyx and Floradine lamps. In an article dated July 18, 1889, of the *Pottery and Glassware Reporter* it announced that: *Dalzell, Gilmore & Leighton Co. hold out at Room 135, with E. D. Gilmore in charge – The 'Royal Arch' lamp, with black base and Floradine bowl, is a very tasteful article, and the 'Daisy,' also with a black base and Floradine bowl, is a pretty specimen too.* The Royal Arch lamp is what is now known to collectors as the Two Post Lamp with either Onyx or Floradine font. The Daisy is the Onyx or Floradine font on the Black Crown lamp base.

The other lamps made in 1889 were the Guthrie and the Oklahoma lines (as in the following illustration). The Guthrie was a stand lamp and the Oklahoma was a two-handled hand lamp.

Pottery and Glassware Reporter, 1889

Hob in Circle Shade, opalescent rubina, 5 1/16" high, 9 1/2"
widest point at top, 4 7/8" base opening, $200+.
Gas lampshade was also made in clear with opalescent and
cranberry with opalescent.

Oklahoma Lamp, clear, 9", $185-250.
Oklahoma Lamp, two handle, clear, 5 3/4", $185-250.
NOTES: Have only found this pattern in clear. Many other sizes
were made.

Hob in Circle Shade, cranberry, 6 1/2" high, 5 3/4" wide top,
4 3/4" wide bottom, $200+.
This hall lampshade was also made in clear glass.

Two Post Lamp with black glass base, blue font, 12 3/4" high to top of collar, 5" square base (not including the feet), $1,500+.
A two-piece lamp with the font in the Bulging Bars design.

Two Post Lamp, black base with a clear font. This font is from the same mold as used with the Findlay Onyx glass as the last pressing mold for the font, $850+.

Priscilla Star Lamp, clear, 5"
to top of collar, $200+.
Priscilla Star Lamp, clear,
$160-190.

Two Post Lamp, clear, 11" high to top of collar, 5" wide, 6 7/8" long, $500+.
Only Clear has been found in this lamp.

The Lamp Machine and the *Force Fit* Collar

On April 11, 1894, was the first mention of the new lamp collars: —*they are about to place on the market a new patent clinched on collar, which they think will take the place of any collar now offered to the trade. They will also have a clinched on molasses can top, something never before attempted, which will be strictly their own and which they believe will be entirely and altogether in it.* These collars for lamps and lids for molasses cans were called "force fit".

We have this information from 1896 but no description: —*The Dalzell, Gilmore & Leighton Co., Findlay, always makes a special drive in plain and decorated lamps, and this year is not a particle behind former years in having several new lines that are different from everything else on the market. A very handsome line of decorations are being put on their goods this season, and a very large sale has been prepared for by starting in on lamps somewhat earlier than usual.* —

Again describing the force fit collars, molasses jug tops, and new machinery, we notice that every time the writers describe the force fit lids and collars, they sound different, but they are one and the same. In *China, Glass & Lamps* on July 6, 1899, it is written that: *Dalzell, Gilmore & Leighton, the Findlay, O, glass manufacturers are at present running two excellent specialties, which are being well made by patented machinery, owned exclusively by this firm. Syrup cans of all sizes, with pressed glass lip, pressed figure and pressed, smooth bottom, are now being made by machinery, by a process which practically revolutionizes the manufacture of this class of ware. In glass lamp manufacture, the firm has perfected machinery which they have been experimenting with for several years, and they are now making one piece, all glass lamps of superior quality, with clinched on, or rather, metal imbedded blown in collars, warranted oil and air tight, and non detachable. These goods have had a large sale wherever introduced, and have given exceptional satisfaction to the trade. Orders for the fall, should be placed early, as these goods are certain to have a very large sale, and will prove leaders in their line.*

Alexis and Nevada Lamps

The Alexis lamp is available in clear and green. It was made in a Handled, flat Hand Lamp; Handled Footed Hand; #1 Stand with #1 Collar; #2 Stand with #1 Collar; #3 Stand with #2 Collar; and #4 Stand with #2 Collar.

The Nevada lamp was made in clear. It was made in a flat handled Hand Lamp; footed handled Hand; #1 Stand; #2, 9" Stand; #3, 9 1/2" Stand; #4, 10" Stand and #5 Stand.

Alexis Lamp, clear, $185-240.
Alexis Lamp, clear with frosted panels, $185-250.

Alexis, Lamp, Hand, 3 1/3", $85-135.
Alexis, Lamp, No. 3, 9 1/2" to the top of the collar, $85-135.
Alexis, Lamp, No. O double handled, 5 7/8" to the top of the collar, $120-150.

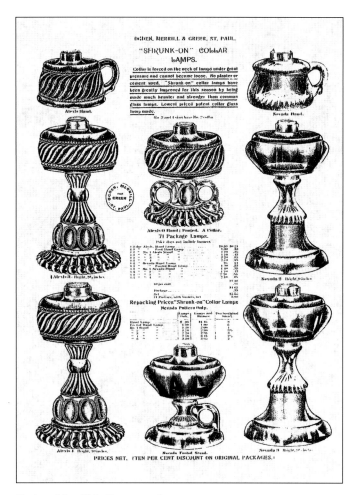

Ogden, Merrill & Greer catalog, 1895

China, Glass & Lamps, May 2, 1901

Dakota and Delaware Lamps

The Dakota and Delaware lamps share the same base but the font is plain on the Delaware. The stems differ in that the stem of the Delaware has the 83D Reeding Bands pattern.

The Dakota Lamp was made in clear and green. This lamp was a lamp that was later made at the Ohio Flint Glass Company. The pattern was also made with the Dracilla and Dorris decorations. Items made were Finger hand lamps in flat and footed; Night Lamp, Dracilla décor; "00" Stand, Dorris décor; "0" Stand; "A" Stand, Dracilla décor; "B" Stand; "C" Stand, Dorris décor; and a Sewing Lamp with #3 Collar and Filler.

The Delaware lamp was manufactured in clear and green. It was sometimes decorated in the Diadem or Duchess styles. It was made in a Sewing Lamp with a #3 Collar and Filler and in the Diadem décor; a Night Lamp; finger, flat Hand; finger, footed Hand, Diadem décor; "00" Stand; "0" Stand, Duchess décor; "A" Stand, "B" Stand, Diadem décor; "C" Stand; and "D" Stand with Duchess décor.

Dakota Lamp, green, 11" high to top of collar, $290-345. Eleven different size lamps were made in the Dakota line.

Dakota Lamp, 9" high, plain, frosted font with some of original paint, tripod base, $185-240. Delaware Lamp, 5 1/2" high miniature lamp with plain frosted font, straight stem base, $185-240. Dakota Lamp, 5 1/2" high miniature lamp with frosted and decorated font, Tripod stem base, $185-240. Eleven different lamps were made in the Delaware line.

Delaware Lamp, clear, 6 1/2" to collar top, $185-240.
Dakota Lamp, Hand, clear, No. 6, No. 1 collar, $195-250.
Dakota Lamp, clear, 6 1/2" to top of collar, $185-240.

Clark Lamp

The Clark Lamp was made in clear glass and clear glass with decorations called Gypsy, Sunset, and Tricolor. The lamps made were a Night Lamp, Flat, handled Hand Lamp, Footed handled Hand Lamp, "00" Stand Lamp, "0" Stand Lamp with Gypsy decor, "A" Stand Lamp, "B" Stand Lamp with Sunset décor, "C" Stand Lamp, and "D" Stand Lamp with Tricolor décor.

Clark Lamp, green, 8 1/2" high, $250-300.
Clark Lamp, clear, 5" high, $185-225.
Clark Lamp, clear, 8 1/2" high, $135-160.

#79D Serrated Teardrop Lamps

The Serrated Teardrop pattern is also known by collectors as Teardrop and Eyewinker. This lamp pattern is also known to have had continued production at the Ohio Flint Glass Company at Lancaster, Ohio.

These lamps were made in clear glass and sometimes found in the Florida décor or the Oregon décor. They were made in a Night Lamp, Handled Footed Hand Lamp, Flat Handled Hand Lamp, "00" Stand Lamp, "0" Stand Lamp, "A" Stand Lamp, "B" Stand Lamp, "C" Stand Lamp with Florida décor, and "D" Stand Lamp with Oregon décor.

No. 79D, Serrated Teardrop Lamp, clear with frosted font, 9" high, $135-165.
No. 79D, Serrated Teardrop Lamp, hand, clear with frosted font, $140-165.
No. 79D, Serrated Teardrop Lamp, miniature, with frosted font, $185-225.

No. 79D, Serrated Teardrop Lamp, green, 9" to top of the #2 collar, $275-325.

Crystal Lamp, clear font, black glass base, 8" high to top of collar, $135-185.
Crystal Lamp, clear font with frosted panels, black glass base, 10 1/4" high to top of collar, $145-175.
NOTES: Many sizes and variations were made in this pattern. Collectors know this lamp as the Crown Lamp.

Elite Lamp

The Elite pattern lamp has been found made in clear, green, and amber. Although this was probably a full line of lamps, the only reference found was to a "0" Hand, two handled, and footed.

Crystal Lamp, a.k.a. Crown

The Crystal lamp was one of the more popular lamps that this firm made. It was somewhat versatile because some of the bases were threaded to accept different fonts including the Six Panel Finecut and Onyx. The ebony foot with the Onyx font was called the Daisy. All of these lamps were available in clear with decorated font, clear decorated foot with plain font, clear font with ruby font, ebony foot with decorated font, clear font with ebony foot, green foot with clear font, clear foot with green font, and all green.

Sizes made are Sewing Lamp, Flat and Footed handled Hand Lamps, Night Lamp, "00", "0", "A", "B", "C", and "D" Stand Lamps.

Crystal Lamp, green, 5 1/4" high to top of collar, $350+.
Crystal Lamp, clear with original paint on frosted panels, 5 1/4" high to top of collar, $245-280.
The painting was done in the decorating department of the Dalzell factory company.

#37D La Grippe,
a.k.a. Convex Rib Lamp

The La Grippe lamp is known to have been made in clear, amber, and blue.

#37D Convex Rib Lamp, blue, 8 7/8" to top of #1 collar, 4 1/8" base, $250-300.

#37D Convex Rib Lamp, amber, 9 1/2" high to top of #1 burner, base 5 1/8", $250-300.
This lamp pattern can also be found in clear.

Sweetheart,
a.k.a. Beaded Heart Lamps.

The Sweetheart lamp has probably as many variations as any lamp that this company made. Production was continued at the Ohio Flint Glass Works at Lancaster, Ohio. The trademark "Krystal" was added to some of the lamps made at Lancaster. While most of the lamps are found with the Dalzell collar, some are found with the standard collar.

To be found are 4 3/4" Night Lamp with a round base in green; 4 3/4" Night Lamp clear; 4 7/8" Night Lamp with a six sided base in green; 4 7/8" Night Lamp in clear with a six sided base; 7 5/8" with a green base, clear font with frosted hearts décor; 5 3/4" Finger Lamp, footed, green; 5 7/8" Finger Lamp footed, clear; 5 7/8" Finger Lamp, footed, clear font with frosted hearts; 2 7/8" Finger Lamp, flat, clear font with frosted inverted hearts; 2 3/4" Finger Lamp, flat, green with inverted hearts; 2 7/8" Finger Lamp, flat, clear with inverted hearts; 7" Stand Lamp, clear, the small font is not in proportion to the base; 7 3/8" Stand Lamp, clear small font not in proportion to the base; 8 1/4" Stand Lamp, green; 9" Stand Lamp, clear; 9 1/2" Stand Lamp, clear; 8 7/8" Stand Lamp, green; 8 3/8" Stand Lamp, clear with frosted hearts and 8 toe base; 8 1/4" Stand Lamp, green with 8 toe base; 10 1/4" Stand Lamp, green font and clear base; 9" Stand Lamp, clear with frosted hearts; 9 1/8" Stand Lamp, clear and 9" Stand Lamp with a green font and clear base. These measurements were made from a private collection and some of the near in size were probably caused by the fit of the collar. These measurements do not include the burner or chimney.

Sweetheart Lamp, 5", green, 6 toed base, $250-300.
Sweetheart Lamp, 5", clear, 6 toed base, $250-300.
Sweetheart Lamp, 5", green, round base, $240-300.

Sweetheart Lamp, clear heart base with green heart font, $250+.

Sweetheart Lamp, green heart base with clear plain font, $250+.

Sweetheart Lamp, green
heart base with clear heart
font, $250+.
Sweetheart Lamp, all green
heart, hand, $200+.

Sweetheart Lamp, hand, flat, green, inverted hearts, 3 3/4" (left), $150-175.
Sweetheart Lamp, hand, footed, green, 5" (center), $165-180.
Sweetheart Lamp, clear with original decoration, 5" (right), $300+.
The miniature lamp on the right was decorated at the factory. The stem is painted red on
the inside and the bottom of the base is painted a midnight blue.

Sweetheart Lamp, clear, heart base, frosted hearts font, $185-200.

Sweetheart Lamp, white opaque, 9 1/4", $250+.
NOTE: Has been reproduced.

Sweetheart Lamp, green heart base with clear frosted hearts font, $250+.
Note: Most Sweetheart lamps have the Dalzell Force Fit collar.

Sweetheart Lamp, green, $185+.

Bibliography

Books

Leighton, George. *Chemist Handbook and Diary*. 1888-1889.

Sanford, Jo & Bob. *Glass Tableware-The Factories and The Men*. Researched Glass Facts, 2000.

Smith, Don. *Findlay Pattern Glass*. Privately Published, 1970.

Factory Catalog

Dalzell, Gilmore & Leighton, circa 1895.

Jobbers' Catalogs

Baltimore Bargain House.
Butler Brothers.
Donaldson, Ogden & Company.
G. Sommers & Company.
Lyon Brothers.
Ogden, Merrill & Greer.
Pitkin & Brooks.
Spelman Brothers.
Wallace & Company.

Trade Journals

American Glassworker, various issues.
China, Glass & Lamps, various issues.
Crockery & Glass Journal, various issues.
Pottery & Glassware Salesman, various issues.

Index

665409

Customer's Order No.			Department		Date 10/16/07		
Name 419-306-1330 cell							
Address							
City, State, Zip							
Sold By	Cash	C.O.D.	Charge	On Acct.	Mdse. Retd.	Paid Out	

QUAN.	DESCRIPTION	PRICE	AMOUNT
1			
2	Waffle goblet		20 —
3	Daffie Fruit spooner		37 50
4			
5			57 50
6			
7			
8	Ms Payne		
9			
10			
11	Findlay Dealer		
12			
13			
14			
15			
16			
17			
18			
19			
Received by			

Adams DC5808

Keep this Slip for Reference